Avoiding a Supply Chain Apocalypse

The Best of Dr. Tom's Advice

by

Dr. Tom DePaoli

DEDICATION
This is dedicated to all purchasing and supply chain
professionals who are fighting in the supply chain
trenches every day.

CONTENTS

INTRODUCTION

Do you find yourself worried about a supply chain apocalypse or meltdown? It is not a question of *if* but of *when*. Tired of the silver bullet one solution flavor-of-the month-answers? So am I, so that's why I wrote and compiled this book! The book will help you master a multi-facetted approach to survive the supply chain apocalypse. Like it or not, we all need to pursue excellence in all aspects of the supply chain, in order to prevent or recover from disasters.

Each chapter of this book presents a collection of my best insights and suggestions to create a world-class supply chain. I provide tips, insights, stories and suggestions to vault your supply chain into unrivaled status. I unabashedly present my best writings on achieving a transformed organization capable of preventing and surviving the supply chain apocalypse. There is no "one answer" to avoid the apocalypse. Supply chain professions need to take a multi-front journey to survive inevitable catastrophes.

I invite the reader to select what is appropriate for their organization and make it happen.

On to chapter one!

1 PURCHASING

1. Pay Purchasing via the New Wave

Most supply chain professionals are familiar with the best practices of a supply chain organization and how to transform purchasing into a lead strategic partner in a company. These usually include a thorough spend analysis to focus on the major areas of materials and services. Another aspect includes the rationalization of suppliers and the formation of a few key partnerships with important suppliers. The institutionalization of a comprehensive sourcing methodology is also crucial. The area that is often overlooked or neglected is the investment in people!

Many purchasing professionals have been rewarded for bureaucratic and tactical behaviors for many years. The culture of risk aversion is prevalent and roles are particularly well-defined and limited. They focus on a particular material or service and become "experts" on these items. Often they work in silos and have no real connection with operations. It is usually not their choice but the expectations of the culture or of their organization.

The retraining of supply chain professionals begins with developing the capability to lead cross-functional teams not only in sourcing, but in process improvement activities such as Lean and Lean Six Sigma. Most need to reach the level of at least a green belt in a process improvement approach, and to reinvent themselves to be total product experts not just a particular material expert. You have to be a product expert to understand the Voice of the Customer (VOC) or what is really important to them. This requires striving to become an expert in an entire industry not just a narrow material. It also requires a dedication to understanding and working with operations. Performance reviews need to be tied into how well they do in predicting the market trends of their particular industry and meeting or exceeding the VOC.

All too often this training is piecemeal, unorganized and uncoordinated. Fortunately there is a comprehensive approach that has been around for 40 years that works in many industries particularly ones where employee knowledge is highly valued like the chemical, oil and process industries. The approach has been called pay-for-skill or pay-for-knowledge. Employees are paid more for each skill or knowledge area that they develop, and demonstrate their proficiency in by job performance. It does require a significant monetary investment by the organization in training employees and the organization evolves to a continuous learning campus. The word campus is critical because many organizations partner with local technical schools or universities to jointly provide the comprehensive training and courses.

Unfortunately many organizations have disinvested in training employees and would rather outsource for many skills or functions. This is deadly to the supply chain concept and process improvement, which must strive to constantly improve the entire supply chain from start to finish without breaks which may or may not be performed better by an outsourced entity. The major objection to the pay-for-skill approach is the cost and the length of time for payback from the employees' improved knowledge. Once in place, however; the power of this employee intellectual capital, and the momentum of continuous improvement, establishes a supply chain centric organization that is nearly impossible to beat competitively.

People transform supply chains and organizations not technology or best practices.

2. Purchasing Can Bootstrap Organizational Transformation!

Purchasing's role in an organization touches across many departments, suppliers, countries, and competitors. This situation requires that purchasing professionals possess excellent communication skills and the ability to quickly adapt to different cultures, perspectives and crises. Transforming your own organization's culture is a grueling challenge. Expecting purchasing to "bootstrap" or use its own resources rather than external help, in organizational transformation, is a demanding goal. Purchasing, however, has many of the qualities and capabilities to act as the prime catalyst for this quest.

In fact many, purchasing organizations have radically changed or reengineered themselves from traditional clerical type organizations. The supply management or supply chain concept is rapidly becoming the norm. This type of change was monumental and transformative. Could purchasing pull the bootstrap off? Most would say highly unlikely, but below are some tactics that could lay the groundwork or accelerate a successful transformation of an organization. Many have been previously used to transform purchasing into supply management.

One of the best ways is by breaking down department silos by involving diverse cross-functional teams in sourcing decisions. Including internal and external customers in as many decisions as possible is a sound empowerment tactic that pays off dramatically. Teamwork in such efforts deepens the understanding of participating employees in the overall purchasing cycle, and helps imbed the concept of total cost of ownership.

Incorporating grassroots efforts to ask internal customers what they want to help simplify purchasing transactions is another powerful tool. People usually appreciate colleagues who try to make their jobs easier and are not afraid of criticism. Making all transactions pain free, fast and intuitive is a strong way to be valued and improve respect for purchasing. Acquiring strong base business knowledge for purchasing, by working side-by-side with production and sales, both improves product knowledge and enhances purchasing professionals' credibility and business perspective. This helps expand the understanding of the voice of the paying customer.

Marketing the importance of purchasing and the supply chain with visible metrics creates a clear focus that others appreciate. Purchasing has to aggressively market their importance to the organization and develop a formal internal marketing plan of their goals. Crafting a long-range purchasing plan that aligns with the organizations vision, mission and strategic plan helps to justify purchasing's efforts to the rest of the organization. Communicating with, as many colleagues on a one-on-one basis should be especially encouraged. This gives purchasing professionals a chance to make their pitch to as many folks as possible and develop strong relationships.

Conducting training and inviting people from other departments to participate helps sell purchasing's goals and metrics. Vital feedback can be obtained on the usefulness of purchasing systems and procedures in such sessions. Finally but most importantly, developing leadership skills and practicing leadership in groups is a good long-term skill-building course of action for all of purchasing. Most experts agree that one skilled leader can turn an organization around. Purchasing needs to be ready with leadership skills to help lead or encourage the organizational transformation process.

Any department would face and probably fail at the nearly impossible task of *bootstrap* transformation of an organization. Purchasing however would be the best place to start the transformation quest and develop the passionate and powerful leaders required to execute it.

3.   Integrate Procurement With Other Departments.

Break down your stovepipe and put procurement folks in other departments. Force them to understand other department needs. Let them go to production meetings and participate. Encourage them to explain to folks what they are doing. Get them on the front lines not the rear bureaucracy. Let them wander about and learn the business. There isn't much real business knowledge learned in a cubicle.

4.   How to Convince Top Executives Of The Value Of Purchasing

Purchasing has continuously demonstrated their impact to the bottom line of an organization. It has been well documented and universality recognized. Then why do many companies refuse to take advantage of this cost saving resource? Why do executives still remain skeptical of purchasing's value? In many organizations purchased materials and services account for over 50% of the cost of goods sold; yet purchasing is often relegated to a bureaucratic mundane dungeon of clerical functions.

Some of the fault lies in purchasing itself. Purchasing personnel are notoriously inept at marketing and selling their ideas and suggestions. They are often a harried bunch running around from firefight to firefight. Most do not even have a good or comprehensive communication plan. They fail to "toot their horn" or market their successes. Purchasing fails to tell their story compellingly and neglects to sell its importance. Other departments either ignore or politely humor purchasing. Purchasing remains the chief cost driver or cost saver for many companies, yet often purchasing is remarkably under resourced and underappreciated.

One-way to sell purchasing's importance is to

empower as many other employees as possible to participate in purchasing especially on cross-functional sourcing teams. Involving as many personnel in constructive purchasing activities educates them on the value and importance of purchasing. This is a bottom-up approach to educating employees on the value of purchasing. It encourages them to contribute their ideas about improving services and products. Purchasing needs to strongly persuade other departments to participate in purchasing processes and decisions. Purchasing all too often fails at what I call the empowerment of employees and internal public relations.

But what can purchasing do about the top executives or top-down? Many executives have stereotype views of purchasing. One of our most successful methods to convince top executives of the value of executives is to encourage direct one-on-one collaboration with executives of your suppliers; especially ones who you are partnering with suppliers who realize the relationship is long-term. Exchanging ideas at this level not only yields great results, but also expedites decisions and removes bureaucratic barriers to success.

The fact is that purchasing also runs its own Research and Development (R&D) department. Suppliers, in collaboration with purchasing, are perhaps the most cost effective R&D function in a company. Jointly they often come up with leaps in technology and transformations in products. When they cooperate they can transform a company and its products. Breakthroughs that occur via this method should receive as much publicity if not more than those developed internally!

In summary getting purchasing valued for its great contribution to revenue; requires both a bottom-up and top-down approach. Empower as many employees as possible to participate in purchasing and solicit their ideas and suggestions. Set up one-on-one executive exchanges with your supplier executives. Finally, systematically create a strong marketing plan to communicate your successes.

5. Benchmarking Via the Shopping-Cart

Many organizations brag about their benchmarking efforts and how good they are at it. I once worked for a large paper company, and a lot of our spending in supply management was for packaging materials involved in the making of toilet tissue and paper towels. I was involved in materials management, plant scheduling, and packaging engineering at the time. Fortunately, all the people involved in these operations reported to me. We were also very fortunate that the plant manager had a materials background and was open to suggestions from us. At first, we went out and tried to get information from various paper institutes, but we found this data to be unwieldy, expensive, and not up-to-date.

Then we just decided to use the shopping cart. We went out to various supermarkets and stores and purchased as many of our competitor's products as we could. We basically dissected them and the materials that they used, looking to see what they had done differently than we had. They were using cheaper materials but had suffered no disconcerting quality drops. Over the years, we had not kept up with the advances in materials. In addition, the process to get new materials approved was unwieldy and required corporate approval. This discouraged almost all the plants from taking risks in the materials area.

We basically changed all our materials specifications to meet or exceed our competitors. In the first year, we saved over $20 million.

6.   Bean Counters Need Corrective Medicine. Make Them Take Their Meds.

Many accountants cannot get beyond price. Their accounting systems cannot measure soft or activity-based costs. They always want to see so-called hard results. They like to audit incessantly. Challenge them to show an ROI or justification of the audit time and energy. Do not let them rule. Keep pushing back on their logic and justification. No one ever brought a share of stock because of a so-called world-class accounting system.

7.   Keep Contract Terms Simple

Why have hundreds of different and complicated terms with suppliers, contracts, and agreements? Suppliers love confusion and nonstandard approaches. Boilerplate whatever you can. Any contract that takes more than thirty days to put in place isn't worth doing. Lawyers, bureaucrats, and fools always think that some-how a contract will "protect" them or the company. Relationships are not built on the thickness of the pages of a massive contract. Trust must come first, not legal "i-dotting." He who hides behind a contract needs high life insurance. Contracts won't save you from adversarial relationships. Contracts, in fact, encourage them. Handshakes encourage trusting relationships.

8.   Talent Trumps All

One of the things I've always done in my personal life (Yes, I have managed to have one!) was coach athletic teams—especially young athletes at all age levels. Nothing makes a coach look more like a genius than talent. This is why when you hire someone in supply management, it's critical that you go after the most-talented people you can get. Certainly the corporate structure and systems can help people succeed, and they play a dramatic role in how successful supply management can be. However, individual talent and drive trumps all. When you have outstanding employees who have ambition to go higher, make sure you give them the tools and training to reach their goal. Take care of your best.

9.   Green Initiatives

Green initiatives are certainly commendable and should be strongly examined by supply management organizations. Customers may in fact demand them from you, so compliance is a good option. It always helps to have green initiatives that save money and waste; here is where Lean can greatly assist you.

10. Inventory My Thoughts

It's essential to work with suppliers and internal customers to reduce inventory levels. Organizations are notoriously lousy inventory managers. Inventory holding costs are always much higher than expected and high inventory causes multiple problems and risk. Each material or service should not have the same inventory strategy. Each deserves a plan based on what the risk is to the organization if an inventory crisis or stock-out occurs. Any initiatives with a supplier that reduces risk should be considered. And remember not all inventory is evil as accountants would have us believe. It can reduce costly risk.

11. Lawyers, Bureaucrats And Fools Always Think Contracts Protect Them

Why have hundreds of different and complicated terms with suppliers, contracts, and agreements? Suppliers love confusion and nonstandard approaches. Boilerplate whatever you can. Any contract that takes more than thirty days to put in place isn't worth doing. Lawyers, bureaucrats, and fools always think that somehow a contract will "protect" them or the company. Relationships are not built on the thickness of the pages of a massive contract. Trust must come first, not legal "i-dotting." He who hides behind a contract needs high life insurance. Contracts won't save you from adversarial relationships. Contracts, in fact, encourage them. Handshakes encourage trusting relationships.

12. Decrease the Total Cost of Ownership By Identifying Cost Drivers First.

Identify your cost drivers first. These are your significant cost factors that drive the cost of a material or service. Then concentrate on the costs that are usually reduced or eliminated by faster cycle time but often forgotten in the rush. Measure areas in which processes got simpler and training costs were decreased.

13. Why A Decrease In Manufacturing Cycle Time Saves Big Dollars.

Keep the tracking of this key parameter simple, to the point, and at a macro level. Show the number of products or widgets made compared to the cost of goods sold. Thus, if you cut cycle time by 50 percent you should make approximately twice as many widgets with about the same cost of goods sold. Realistically, the cost of goods sold will have to increase, but cycle-time reduction can radically hold down the rate of increase.

14. Purchasing's Internal Customer-Client Satisfaction Is Critical.

Start an ongoing internal customer focus team to evaluate the performance and service of purchasing. Periodically use surveys of internal customers, final customers, and suppliers to obtain valuable feedback and direction on how to reduce cycle time. Always include in customer-satisfaction surveys the question, "Has the response time to your request increased, decreased, or stayed the same?" Don't forget face-to-face feedback meetings.

15. Manufacturing And Administrative Flexibility Are Key To Reducing Cycle Time.

When measuring flexibility in the manufacturing process, focus on reducing the total number of parts. Purchasers can track increases in the number of easily obtainable standardized parts and services with zero lead-time. Also, suppliers can pre-assemble and assist in these types of efforts.

Don't neglect the administrative cycle time in a purchasing department -- whether you work for a manufacturing company or a service organization. Purchasers can set cycle-time standards in their departments and streamline all procedures to speed things up. For example, procurement cards and system-purchasing systems can help reduce cycle time.

19. Should Purchasing Use 360 Degree Performance Feedback?

As we know, 360-degree performance feedback is an evaluation method that incorporates feedback from a large cross section of workers including peers, subordinates, customers and supervisors. This technique would seem perfect for purchasing in this era of cross functional teams and multidimensional relationships in the supply chain.

Not so fast. This method should not be used or tied to pay or merit pay especially for purchasing. It is fine for giving feedback to an individual on the impressions that they convey to people, but all too often it has become a popularity contest. Any purchasing professional who is worth their salt, knows that purchasing is not a place where one becomes very well-liked. Difficult and controversial decisions are the norm not the exception.

Purchasing is also an area where the pace is frenetic; fire-fighting is all too often prevalent and quick decisions are needed to prevent major shutdowns. Fast direct decisions are the norm rather than slow diplomatic ones. Often purchasing professionals are forced to be executers or quick problem solvers. They have little time for being corporate relators or engaging in "water cooler" social exercises. The emphasis is on solving the latest crises, not social networking. Although generation M is enamored with relationships via social networking, purchasing is often driven by multiple crises and has little time for such digital schmoozing. Their focus on solving the crisis is often misinterpreted by peers as being cold, harried, non-relating and impersonal. Thus feedback from a 360-degree evaluation must be tempered by this purchasing reality.

In summary, a 360-degree evaluation for a purchasing professional has some use in providing relevant feedback on how the purchasing professional is viewed by peers and does give some first impression detail. This feedback must be tempered however by the crisis reality of the purchasing department. It should never be used for performance or merit pay. In addition, realize that there is no empirical evidence that the 360-degree approach is superior or more effective than other approaches.

20. How Can a Purchasing Professional Get "Street Cred" in Their Company?

Most purchasing professionals have skills in purchasing, negotiations, and the materials or services that they buy. Many have certifications. They have dutifully enhanced their skills in all these areas and pursue continuing education. Unfortunately what many organizations value are operations skills, or what they know about the core business and the customers.

Some purchasing professionals have come up from the ranks or gained operational experience in other internal jobs in the company and they are fine, but most often this is not the case. The challenge for the purchasing professional is how to gain this respected credibility when they are often swamped with other priorities and crises.

One of the best sources may be a supplier or distributer who is willing to take the time and discuss your competition. You will be surprised about how much knowledge they have. They are especially valuable discussing the Voice of the Customer (VOC) and your customers' concerns. Often they supply your customers.

Since many purchasing professionals have a material or service specialty, my advice is to get out on the shop floor or area where your folks actually use the material that you source. For example, when I was in charge of purchasing wires for a papermaking machine, I went out to the paper machines and actually observed the crew tear off a new wire and put on the new one. Yes, it was wet and hot but I soon got a sound understanding of their issues and concerns. Another way is to actually go on service calls with your service technicians and observe and listen. This is usually unfiltered and sometimes you receive unflattering feedback from the customer.

One of the best ways is to conduct internal training with the purchasing department. Have engineering or customer service give you training on your products and how they work. Have them gear the training to the purchasing department. When I was in purchasing, we asked them to design a training manual targeted to us and they gladly did this by just modifying the existing one. The best instructors know how to make the complicated simple and present the customers' point of view. One of the best courses I attended was Papermaking for the Non-Papermaker which avoided all the confusing technical argot. Another way is to have department meetings where fellow purchasing professionals share what new knowledge they have gained about your products and services. This is an especially good approach because it is relatively non-threatening.

Nothing flatters operational or shop floor personnel more than going right where they work, and asking them to train you about their job and duties. Showing a genuine interest goes a long way in establishing your credibility and getting their cooperation in the future on purchasing projects such as sourcing.

Finally getting "street cred" is not an instantaneous process. Respect does not occur overnight. You will have to take the time and effort to build up your reputation as a purchasing professional who can be trusted more, because they truly understand the core business.

21. Purchasing Professionals Need Teamwork That Builds on Their Strengths

Purchasing departments are usually close-knit organizations that must endure constant crises, challenges and rapidly changing supply chains. The need for teamwork is especially important.

In a previous blog, Purchasing Leaders Need a Combination of Exceptional One-Off Leadership Skills, I noted that a purchasing leader needs to be trusted and trust his team members. Having unimpeachable integrity is key. I then listed various tactics to accomplish this. More noteworthy, usually because of a lack of resources, and constant firefighting, a purchasing leader must carefully coach his professionals. One method to do this is by placing them in areas where then can succeed and not fail.

One tool that I have used to discover what purchasing professionals are good at, or what makes them stand out, is the Gallup organization's StrengthsQuest. This testing instrument helps people discover their strengths (also called themes) and appropriately use them. Each individual has five strengths identified. There are 34 total identified themes or strengths. These are placed in four domains: Executing, influencing, relationship-building and strategic-thinking. For a team, it is essential to share these strengths so that team members can realize what they are good at and what their teammates have as their strengths. The purchasing leader can then assign purchasing tasks to people based on their strengths and what they are not only good at, but likely actually prefer these tasks. In other words play to the strengths of your team members.

Let me give an example. One of my strengths was identified as strategic. The general description of this theme is: People exceptionally talented in the strategic theme create alternative ways to proceed. Faced with any given scenario, they can quickly spot the relevant patterns and issues.

A more specific description about me is: "It's very likely that you might generate certain types of ideas quickly. Occasionally you draw links between facts, events, people, problems, or solutions. You may present numerous options for consideration. Perhaps your innovative thinking fosters ongoing dialogue between and among associates, committee members, teammates, or classmates. Because of your strengths, you might have a knack for identifying problems. You might generate alternatives for solving them. Sometimes you consider the pros and cons of each option. Perhaps you factor into your thinking prevailing circumstances or available resources. Maybe you feel life is good when you think you may be choosing the best course of action.

"Chances are good that you may be viewed by some people as an innovative and original thinker.

Perhaps your ability to generate options causes others to see there is more than one way to attain an objective. Now and then, you help certain individuals select the best alternative after having weighed the pros and cons in light of prevailing circumstances or available resources. Instinctively, you sometimes know what has gone wrong. You try to uncover facts.

"Perhaps you are not intimidated by an overwhelming amount of information. Like a detective, you might sort through it, attempting to identify pieces of evidence. Following a few leads, you might begin to see the big picture. Maybe you generate schemes for solving the problem. You might choose the best option after considering some of the prevailing circumstances, available resources, or desired outcomes. By nature, you may see solutions before other people know there is a problem. You might start formulating answers before your teammates, coworkers, or classmates understand the question. Sometimes you generate numerous ideas before sorting to the one that makes the most sense in a particular situation."

This strategic strength or theme has done me well in my purchasing career. I focused more on strategic relationships with suppliers, creative projects with suppliers, long-term strategic plans, and being prepared with options when things go wrong. As we all know, in purchasing things unfortunately, do sometimes tend to go wrong.

But enough about me!

The point that I am making is that a purchasing leader should take the time to understand the strengths, skills and talents of their professional team and mesh them into the goals and tasks of the organization. The key point is to give purchasing professionals clear chances to succeed by using their strengths, rather that berate them for their weaknesses.

StrengthsQuest is an excellent tool, which I recommend, to help the purchasing leader build stronger and more powerful teams.

23. Can Appreciative Inquiry Work For Purchasing?

Most purchasing professionals have never heard of appreciative inquiry. It is a systematic discovery process to search for what is best or positive in an organization or its strengths. These strengths are then improved upon to create an even stronger and more dynamic organization. Implementing change remains positive and thus springs from an organization's strengths, not its weaknesses, or deficiencies.

All too often in my purchasing career, I have experienced a new purchasing leader or consultant, who comes from an outside company, then sweeps into a purchasing department and castigates purchasing professionals for, "doing everything wrong, unlike their former company, that did everything right." This negative reactive approach to change often results in people becoming even more resistant to change. Traditional reactive methods to implementing change emphasize fixing what is broken or weak in an organization. This approach almost never works and causes even more fear.

One of the tools of appreciative inquiry is the sharing of stories about an organization. Employees are asked to describe a time when they were really engaged and excited about their work. Employees are asked to list what was great or memorable about the time. The themes or actions that the organization used are carefully studied and grouped. Common themes of these stories may evolve or confirm a major strength of an organization. These strengths then become skill springboards from which the organization needs to use and embellish.

I have previously discussed the storytelling techniques in a blog at My Purchasing Center titled Use the Storytelling Method to Train Supply Chain Professionals.
As a review, here are some of the advantages of storytelling:
• The brain stores information by stories.
• Stories are humanizing and stimulate creativity.
• Storytelling improves listening skills.
• Storytelling builds a team culture.
• It encourages collaboration.

Appreciative inquiry takes storytelling to the next level. The memorable stories and positive results become the dynamic building blocks of an organization's competitive edge. It makes the vision or mission become actualized or reach their full potential!

Here is an example. One of the strengths of a purchasing organization that I led was sourcing and the use of cross-functional teams. The vast majority of the team members felt good about the sourcing decision and the transition plan to the selected supplier. A systematic methodology was used and modified as needed. Team members were well equipped to defend the selection and present the reasoning to other non-team members. Most members could defend and justify the selection and did it consistently and with enthusiasm. To my surprise the non-purchasing team members were even better at justifying the selection. The metrics almost always supported the supplier selection.

I, like many purchasing professionals, was initially very skeptical of the appreciative inquiry approach. Who has the time for it? Purchasing spends an inordinate amount of time fixing what is broken like expediting orders, handling bad quality parts, fixing bad suppliers, chasing down supply chain interruptions and overall upsets. These are all in the realm of fixing what is broke. The fact is that purchasing spends too much time as a firefighters putting out fires. Living in this type of hectic atmosphere or culture does not encourage a different positive approach to change. In fact, it encourages skepticism and the avoiding of risk.

In conclusion, appreciative inquiry can be a useful approach for positive change in purchasing. The challenge to purchasing is to make the time to discover the strengths of the purchasing organization. It requires patience and the gathering of memorable stories. Purchasing should build on its strengths rather than tear down its image by constantly fixing what is "broke." In purchasing you are what you are perceived. Too often purchasing is viewed, as the harried firefighter who can never put out all the fires.

Appreciative inquiry is a good approach to start to change this negative traditional image.

24. Can Purchasing Bootstrap and Lead the Transformation of An Organization?

Purchasing's role in an organization touches across many departments, suppliers, countries, and competitors. This situation requires that purchasing professionals possess excellent communication skills and the ability to quickly adapt to different cultures, perspectives and crises.

Transforming your own organization's culture is a grueling challenge. Expecting purchasing to "bootstrap" or use its own resources rather than external help, in organizational transformation, is a demanding goal. Purchasing, however, has many of the qualities and capabilities to act as the prime catalyst for this quest.

In fact many, purchasing organizations have radically changed or reengineered themselves from traditional clerical type organizations. The supply management or supply chain concept is rapidly becoming the norm. This type of change was monumental and transformative.

Could purchasing pull the bootstrap off? Most would say highly unlikely, but below are some tactics that could lay the groundwork or accelerate a successful transformation of an organization. Many have been previously used to transform purchasing into supply management.

One of the best ways is by breaking down department silos by involving diverse cross-functional teams in sourcing decisions. Including internal and external customers in as many decisions as possible is a sound empowerment tactic that pays off dramatically. Teamwork in such efforts deepens the understanding of participating employees in the overall purchasing cycle, and helps imbed the concept of total cost of ownership.

Incorporating grassroots efforts to ask internal customers what they want to help simplify purchasing transactions is another powerful tool. People usually appreciate colleagues who try to make their jobs easier and are not afraid of criticism. Making all transactions pain free, fast and intuitive is a strong way to increase value of and improve respect for purchasing. Acquiring strong base business knowledge for purchasing, by working side-by-side with production and sales, both improves product knowledge and enhances purchasing professionals' credibility and business perspective. This helps expand the understanding of the voice of the paying customer.

Marketing the importance of purchasing and the supply chain with visible metrics creates a clear focus that others appreciate. Purchasing has to aggressively market its importance to the organization and develop a formal internal marketing plan of its goals.

Crafting a long-range purchasing plan that aligns with the organization's vision, mission and strategic plan helps to justify purchasing's efforts to the rest of the organization. Communicating with as many colleagues on a one-on-one basis should be especially encouraged. This gives purchasing professionals a chance to make their pitch to as many folks as possible and develop strong relationships.

Conducting training and inviting people from other departments to participate helps sell purchasing's goals and metrics. Vital feedback can be obtained on the usefulness of purchasing systems and procedures in such sessions.

Finally, but most important, developing leadership skills and practicing leadership in groups is a good long-term skill-building course of action for all of purchasing. Most experts agree that one skilled leader can turn an organization around. Purchasing needs to be ready with leadership skills to help lead or encourage the organizational transformation process.

Any department would face and probably fail at the nearly impossible task of bootstrap transformation of an organization. Purchasing however would be the best place to start the transformation quest and develop the passionate and powerful leaders required to execute it.

25. Market Your Purchasing Successes with the Use of Storyboards

Purchasing professionals need to realize that they must not only market their purchasing strategies but their successes. Many purchasing professionals neglect to create a marketing plan for their organization. I use the term marketing plan synonymously with communication plan.

Some of the goals and techniques of your marketing-communication plan should be to educate top management on your strategic plans, publish results of supplier performance and surveys, publish internal customer survey results, educate personnel on purchasing and supply chain principles, emails, hold roundtables, hold town meetings, use social media, utilize newsletters, use a supply chain specific web page, monthly letters, and announcement of successes.

Storyboards are a great way to market your successes. Storyboards require you to be disciplined in your message and fully understand your results and assertions. You must limit your words and concentrate on the essentials. Thus you must communicate explicitly and right to the point for your audience. You need to strip away the technical argot and make sure the audience can easily grasp what you have accomplished, even with a very limited knowledge of purchasing.

Storyboards should adhere to a lean principle of visibility. Storyboards must be understood quickly with the maximum use of graphics, not words, spreadsheets or numbers. This is not an easy task, as a consultant we would often spent hours and days trying to accomplish this with a storyboard. Obviously purchasing often does not have the talent (full-time illustrator) or resources to do this meticulously, but this is intended to be a guide.

There is no one catch-all formula or template for storyboards. Often how you employ them and your particular style depends on the culture and communication norms of your organization. The important aspect is to make sure that you communicate your successes in a manner that can be readily understood by both purchasing and non-purchasing personnel. Think of storyboards as intelligent commercials that must be brief, easily remembered and upbeat.

I have provided an example of a storyboard that we used to communicate a purchase order success story. The organization that it was used in was very heavily into Lean Six Sigma, Kaizens and the DMAIC methodology (Define-Measure-Analyze-Improve-Control). We used this familiar DMAIC format to help people understand and follow what we did. It still has too many words and numbers but we needed to ensure people realized the scope of what we had accomplished. The storyboard was well received and readily understood by employees. I highly recommend purchasing and supply chain professionals consider using storyboards to communicate your successes.

26. Strategies to Limit Backdoor or Maverick Buying

Backdoor or maverick buying is a perplexing problem that plagues many purchasing organizations. The methods to counteract this behavior are highly dependent upon the cultural climate and ethical standards of your organization. There is no universal solution. People's behaviors are influenced by consequences. If there are no consequences for backdoor buying the behavior will continue and grow. Some of my suggestions are drastic, others are more reasonable. Purchasing professionals must use their judgment to select the appropriate actions that fit their particular organization.

An important aspect to solving this issue is to

remain objective and to try to gather data on the costs of backdoor buying. These could include lost discounts, lost rebates, and extra transactional work by purchasing and others. Many purchasing organizations know the average transactional cost of a regular transaction with an approved supplier. Try to calculate the extra cost with an unapproved supplier. Always control your emotions when discussing this issue.

Here are some reasonable tactics to create an organizational atmosphere and climate that helps discourage backdoor buying. In my experience the biggest offender is usually the engineering department. So involve engineering in cross-functional supplier selection teams and standardization initiatives. Make them a stakeholder in approving suppliers. Get the vice president of engineering on board with OEM (Original Equipment Manufacturer) standardization and have them participate in OEM standardization processes.

Consider establishing a policy of no gifts or gratuities to be accepted from suppliers by both purchasing and all other employees (zero tolerance). This discourages lunchtime promises or promise buys to suppliers by non-purchasing employees. Another alternative is to have purchasing have their own modest budget to entertain, socialize and conduct work sessions with suppliers.

Get your compliance employees on board with your policy i.e., your legal department and accounting. Craft an approved supplier only purchasing policy and make it clear that unauthorized purchases will not be honored by accounts payable. Keep the list of approved suppliers visible and updated. Use your software safeguard controls to limit buying privileges and cross reference the approved supplier list. Many purchase cards can be limited to specific approved suppliers and or categories of goods. Meet with your approved preferred suppliers and ask them to use the grapevine to communicate any unauthorized purchases directly to you. Most will gladly do this.

One of the most effective drastic actions occurred when I worked for a global chemical company. The company had just spent over $200 million on a worldwide ERP system. The CEO sent out a strong memo saying that all purchases must be made on the ERP system and only from the approved suppliers in the ERP system. Employees were required to use the new ERP system. The very first day four employees went off system to purchase some items from a non-approved supplier. The CEO personally fired them and publicized the results of the incident to all employees. Needless to say there were no more such purchases.

Do your networking and informal work before you institute your policy. Meet one-on-one with stakeholders or in small meetings to explain your reasons for your policy and get their buy-in before you roll it out.

Establishing a policy against backdoor buying requires some deft maneuvering by purchasing that judges the culture of your organization. Instituting the appropriate policy will help reduce backdoor buying. More important, you must enforce the policy and reprimand employees who violate it. A backdoor buying policy unenforced, is meaningless.

Avoiding a Supply Chain Apocalypse

2 RELATIONSHIPS

1. Why Women Are Better At Relationships

Women are far superior in relationship building and getting people to cooperate and problem solve together. Negotiation at the strategic level should not be considered a "contest" or sporting event. Unfortunately, many men view it in this manner. At the strategic level it is more about making breakthroughs together and getting a unique competitive advantage, that you're paying customers cannot ignore. You desire what I call "leapfrog" breakthroughs, not wins and losses. Again, we do not want to stereotype, but from my experiences, most women have far superior relationship building skills. Don't confuse this with the old fashion beat up your opponent adversarial negotiation methodology. This is appropriate for some situations. But it rarely results in breakthroughs. I explain this in more detail in my books.

2. It's About Relationships First And Foremost

Purchasing is the art of building relationships. It is not about negotiations, transactions, industry knowledge, market knowledge, know-how or technology. It is all about building strong relationships and gaining the trust of suppliers, customers, and colleagues. Nothing else comes close to building relationships in importance for successful purchasing. A purchasing professional must be able to build relationships or they are about as useless as a screen door on a submarine. They may need to pursue another career. Do not spend inordinate amounts of money on so called purchasing technical training unless a strong foundation of relationships is well underway. You cannot fake relationships. You cannot legislate it. Purchasing professionals need to live it and commit to it. Integrity in relationships will always carry the day, impress suppliers, scare the competition, and let you sleep well at night. Educational credentials look good, and certifications are impressive but nothing makes a purchasing professional more effective than developing strong relationships and being true to their word. Spending more time on relationships almost always pays off for all participants. Once trust or relationships are broken they are nearly impossible to repair, so don't neglect them or underestimate their criticality. You will not be able to dig yourself out of any of the deep holes that you dig by dishonest relationships. Smoozing is a lot easier than shoveling. Honesty builds respect.

3. How to Get Employees to Trust You

There is no easy way to get employees to trust you. One of things that I've always done is to make sure that I do what I told them I was going to do. Nothing impresses employees more than keeping your word. Another good tactic to use is to always admit your mistakes and do not try to cover them up. Employees appreciate when you invest the time and effort to train them. Make sure you have a training plan for all of your employees. Try to behave ethically, employees expect you to lead by example and to live by your word. Communicate to them daily if possible in use as many different channels of communication as you can.

Remember some people have preferred channels for communication. Take the time to understand what they do and respect what they do.

One of the things that I always did was sitting down with my employees and not only watching how they do their jobs but actually have them teach me how to do their job, then go out and actually do some of it. This really grounds you as a boss. You get a good understanding of the aspects of their job and what they go through every day. If I work for a company that had well documented work practices, I would read these before I sat down with the employee. This gave me a good background to learn more rapidly. It also showed the employee that I was very interested in what they do.

4. The Choir Does Not Need A Sermon

Most supply management folks want to do the right thing and be more strategic rather than tactical. Strategy is concerned with long term fixes, innovation and vision. Tactics is usually the day-to-day firefighting. Antiquated processes and systems drag them down and inhibit any creativity. Certainty keeping their morale high during a transformation process is essential. Unmotivated or disgruntled people do not innovate well. Over-killing with strategy, which is borderline ideology, will produce skepticism and distrust. Let them learn and make mistakes that will teach them even more. Make sure they network with each other and share lessons learned. You need to make them grizzled veterans quickly.

5. Build Relationships with Suppliers For Dramatic Results

Most purchasing professionals are familiar with the usual quantifiable supplier metrics and measures. Sophisticated computerized tracking programs exist to measure these traditional performance factors. There are nontraditional supplier metrics/activities that can help not only to rate a supplier, but also to build much stronger supplier relationships.

First, you can learn a lot about a supplier by visiting its sites and just observing the cleanliness of the plant, morale of the employees and overall sense of urgency of the operation. For most purchasing professionals the challenge is finding the time to conduct these visits and conducting them skillfully. A planned and disciplined site visit schedule can help overcome this obstacle. Every site visit should be documented and have a report filed for future comparison. It should always include the subjective impressions of the visiting purchasing professional.

How a supplier performs in disaster recovery (yours) provides an invaluable lesson of their commitment to you. We once had an electrical supplier lead the effort to restore power to one of our chemical plants after a devastating hurricane. The employees at the plant still marvel about how well they performed. These out-of-the-ordinary efforts should result in strong recognition to the supplier and possible increased sourcing from them. It can lead to another strong relationship-building activity of pre-planning for possible disaster-recovery with not one but multiple suppliers before they happen. Often vulnerabilities can be anticipated and dealt with appropriately.

Participation in process improvement efforts, such as Lean Six Sigma, is another strong builder of supplier commitment. Supplier input and suggestions to specifications changes for a part or service are invaluable. Many suppliers are eager to provide suggestions to help improve your process. Turnabout is fair play and you should participate in their process improvement and process-mapping efforts with their products, especially those that you purchase.

We once had a supplier increase the life of a critical part that cost us $35,000, from 30 days to 250 days. It did take two years of painstaking work and experimentation. Eventually, because we dramatically reduced the dollar value of our purchases (with the supplier's help), we hired the supplier as an ongoing technical service consultant. They had learned so much about our production process and now had the capability of providing invaluable insights.

Sharing of R&D efforts and data systems is another high level of cooperation that can lead to mutual benefits. Obviously this requires an extremely high level of trust and collaboration. It quickly reveals the IT capabilities of the supplier and its ability to respond to your needs. Many suppliers are often willing to share industry and market research with customers along with forecasting techniques. Take advantage of their expertise in these areas.
These types of relationship building metrics/activities can lead to dramatic gains for both the supplier and the purchasing professional. A purchasing professional

needs to realize that most are not quick fixes but require a concerted and tough long term effort. The payback can be dramatic.

6. Roadmap to Supplier Relationship Success

Supplier relationship management is the process of developing a deep collaborative partnership or alliance with a supplier. The supplier becomes a true and trusted business partner. The relationship is characterized by open disclosure, cultural calibrating and joint beneficial projects. Ultimate alliance partnerships are at the highest level. These should be reserved for a few suppliers, with criteria for selection being that the supplier can help a company obtain a dominant competitive advantage.

Use a five-stage model or roadmap to develop your relationships with suppliers. The deeper the relationship desired the further along the roadmap one progresses. Suggested activities for the supplier are listed at each stage of the relationship. Of course there must be willingness for the supplier to enter into a relationship and clear quantifiable metrics must be used. Trust is not always easily quantifiable. Good luck with the roadmap and your relationship building!

Stages of Supplier Relationship Building Initiating Stage

This stage is characterized by initial meetings where small tasks are attempted or reviewed. The process is primarily task related and the mutual needs are slowly being discovered. This is the stage were socialization takes place with a supplier via visits, dinners, mutual presentations and sharing more information. This is a low key problem-solving stage. No major decisions are made. The emphasis is on sharing information and checking if the relationship can become deeper. Examples of activities are:

• Sharing understandings of administrative and IT procedures.

• Understanding procurement rules, transaction flows invoice rules, purchase order format. Minimizing the upsets before they can happen.

• Comparing some base data, like on time deliveries. Discussing the differences in transactions and discrepancies.

Experimenting Stage

This stage starts to intensify the relationship. The emphasis here is to experiment with problem-solving activities that are fun. They should have a low risk of self-disclosure. The purpose is to discover if a deeper partnership is possible.

Examples of activities are:

• Each partner maps the other's actual supply chain. This in a learning activity and not meant to be critical. Potential partners present their understanding to each other. Both parties increase learning during the exercise. We developed a visualization technique in the paper industry where the group imagined they were a wood chip and then discussed all the transforms and processes that were happening to the wood chip until it transformed into a toilet paper roll. The "how" the supplier chain is presented, such as props, methods are up to both parties' discretion.

• The administrative, transactional or paperwork supply chain is mapped in a similar manner.

• One mutual low-risk problem is agreed to and a joint mini-case analysis conducted. Topics such as electronic communication, pay-on-receipt, receiving etc., are compared and parties agree to a common solution or understanding. This is usually an issue where both parties are close but a few loose ends need to be tied.

Intensifying Stage

At this stage trust and support with open disclosure start to become the norm. Feedback on the status of the relationship is frequent. Rules of relationship behavior are developed.

Examples of activities include:

• Some mutual cost sharing and cost driver sharing information.

• Intensified effort to streamline administrative bottlenecks in supply chain and to eliminate all non-value adding discrepancies so both parties can focus on more important issues and the relationships. Eliminating the "irritants".

• Mutual work load or administrative reduction agreements and negotiations on any stickler performance measures.

• More thorough reviews that concentrate on new mutually beneficial projects.

Integrating Stage

Both parties start to recognize the special relationship and exchange symbols of the relationship. Terms like "us" and "we" become the norm. The partners tend to rely on each other more and start to integrate processes.

Examples of activities include:

• Full financial disclosure.

• Exchanges of corporate symbols such as pins, awards etc.

• The integration of some business processes. One partner may lead the sharing of a process or skill with the other partner such as assisting in electronic communications setup. Actual assets may be shared.

• Some mutual marketing or campaigns are started.

• Employee sharing and exchange of executives becomes standard.

Bonding Stage

This is the final stage of coming together and the deepest relationship.

Examples of activities include:

• Joint R&D ventures and sharing of innovations all along the supply chain simultaneously as they are discovered.

• Full design stage collaboration.

• Mutual executive development and career path plans.

• Sharing of IT resources and customers information.

Follow this roadmap to ensure SRM success.

3 SUPPLY MANAGEMENT

1. Supply Chain Hero's

Supply chain professionals are often ridiculed and lambasted especially when things go wrong in the supply chain. Crises however are important times to engage the supplier on what went wrong and to prevent future occurrences. Mistakes are gems in the supply chain and often result in improved process mapping of the failed process. Take advantage of failure to create a new process. Become a hero.

2. Mega Negotiations Ground Rules

These were the ground rules we established for a $5 billion dollar bid of supplier work for major expansion of chemical plants.

1. There would be only one round of bids. We urged the suppliers to give the bid their best shot. We didn't have the time to manage multiple bids.

2. We announced that we would, in many cases, narrow down the areas where we had two preferred suppliers to one, unless we had a good business reason for keeping two.

3. Although we had negotiated some significant total-cost-of-ownership savings in the current contracts, we were open to enhancements from the suppliers and distributors.

4. We told the suppliers that we would not accept their standard spare parts packages as we had in the past. We would challenge their typical spares packages, but would be especially open to creative ways of them controlling and managing the spares at minimal or no cost to us.

5.   OEMs (Original Equipment Manufacturers) could work with distributors to propose any additional creative services to provide us.

3.   Have Supply Management People Attend Production Meetings It Works!

One of the first things that I had my supply management people do was to attend production meetings that took place every day in the plant. I required them to attend the meeting's which were often conducted early and before many staff personnel normally arrived in the plant. I myself, when I worked in production, had heard various staff functions being criticized by production personnel and basically bad-mouthed. My logic to my people was that if they are going to bad-mouth you, you should be present to hear it, or defend yourself, or take action to correct what they were complaining about. What shortly happened is that the production people soon realized that informing supply management people of potential problems gave us a much better chance of helping them with spare parts or maintenance orders. It also eliminated any of the normal message hand-off noise that accompanied many of their requests and demonstrated that we had a sense of urgency to help solve their problems. We also brought in supplier experts to help with technical problems and issues that arose. Soon my people were accepted as contributing members of the production team.

4. Let Your Employees Out-Dream You

Get your employees to out-dream you. Get them to

state what the Supply Management department of the future will look like. Take their dreams and build on the dreams. When they out dream you, you know you are on the way to <u>Supply Management Shanghai-La</u>. Visualize future behaviors and performance. Verbalize them. Verbalize world-class behaviors. It helps immensely to ground folks in what you are trying to accomplish. You want them to soar and dream! Let them.

7. Book Review Wayne Hurlbert

"This book is a summary of many of the lessons that I learned in my supply management and management career", writes Management Program Director at Marian University, and Principal and CEO of Apollo Solutions, Tom DePaoli, in his engaging and practical lesson filled book Common Sense Supply Management: Tales From The Supply Chain Trenches. The author describes best practices, Lean Six Sigma, and information based negotiations through the medium of stories as superior teaching and idea retention vehicle.

Tom DePaoli recognizes that supply chain management remains the basic framework of most organizations. As a result, the author provides insights into how to transform that crucial element into a powerful competitive advantage. While the management of the supply chain is complex undertaking for most companies, Tom DePaoli shares his experience by way of readily understood and remembered stories. As with any other aspect of the overall business, supply chain management is fundamentally based in business and personal relationships. Because of the complexity nature of supply chains, the author presents the premise that a s successful supply chain manager is able to develop and maintain many simultaneous relationships across many organizations and different people.

Tom DePaoli recognizes the primary importance of business relationships, and their critical role in navigating the complexities of supply management. The stories shared by the author present this concept very well. Indeed, the focus of the entire book is on the interaction and relationships between people. The concepts of best practices, Lean Six Sigma, and information based negotiations all share a common human relationship element. Tom DePaoli offers a proven multi-layered approach to finding, sourcing, and working effectively with suppliers.

Perhaps even more importantly, the author cautions business people about the problems that arise through international sourcing strategies. For negotiating better terms with suppliers, while developing strong personal relationships, the author shares his real world tested strategies and tactics. At the same time, Tom DePaoli provides an understandable and useful system of metrics for measuring the effectiveness of the entire supply management system.

For me, the power of the book is how Tom DePaoli combines the human aspects of supply management with a comprehensive strategic approach to developing an effective management system. The author shares his personal experience in the real world of supply management, and as a result, offers practical and readily applied knowledge and information. Tom DePaoli also shares his concepts of negotiation that apply lessons learned in actual negotiation situations.

Instead of automatically recommending a win-win negotiation strategy, the author presents an effective alternative in the form of an information-based technique. This contrast is one of the many valuable lessons offered in the book. Unlike many books on the topic, the author shares an accessible and readily applied approach to metrics and measurement. The chapters in the book are short and contain useful and relevant stories of the principles in action. The book is a handy reference that can be referred to as a guide to improving any supply management system.

I highly recommend the very accessible and hands on book Common Sense Supply Management: Tales From The Supply Chain Trenches by Dr. Tom DePaoli, to any business leaders, entrepreneurs, and negotiators seeking a practical and no nonsense guide to improving any supply management process. This book will transform your supply management system from the ordinary to the outstanding, while boosting your overall bottom line.

8. Marian University Business Professor Authors Book, Common Sense Supply Management

Fond du Lac, Wis. - A Marian University business professor recently announced his authorship of a new book that examines the world of supply chain management.

Dr. Tom DePaoli

Dr. Tom DePaoli, director of the Management
Program in the School of Business & Public Safety, is
the author of "Common Sense Supply Management:
Tales from the Supply Chain Trenches" that was
released in September. In a reader-friendly, storytelling
format, the book uses real life examples to discuss what
goes right, and often wrong, in the supply chain
management trenches.

"Supply management covers more breadth and
depth than any other discipline in an organization," said
DePaoli. "It is the art of building multiple
relationships."

DePaoli's book advances the field of supply
management to tackle best practices, Lean Six
Sigma and information-based negotiations. He includes
an extensive chapter on planning and strategy that
prepares the supply management professionals for his
multi-dimensional approach to suppliers, offers proven
tactics for testing and sourcing suppliers and discusses
the possible pitfalls of using international sourcing.

DePaoli earned his doctoral degree California Coast
University, and his master's degree in management
from the University of Notre Dame Graduate
School of Business. DePaoli has published extensively,
with previous publications including "Common Sense
Purchasing."

9. Amazon Reviews Of Common Sense Supply Management

This review is from: Common Sense Supply
Management: Tales From The Supply Chain Trenches
In his new book, Common Sense Supply

Management--Tales from the Supply Chain Trenches, Dr. Tom DePaoli shares experiences from his career as a procurement professional and offers how-to-advice for transforming a sourcing operation.

The tales consist of easy-to-read short stories on such topics as negotiations, building relationships, benchmarking, supplier relationship management, and e-procurement.

In one, DePaoli relates why beating suppliers constantly doesn't work. In another, he explains how managers can earn trust of their employees. A third looks at why women excel at managing relationships with suppliers.

"Here's what I've done that works," DePaoli tells My Purchasing Center of the collection that he describes as enjoyable to read. "I tell the story. But I don't give a lesson. Readers can figure it out on their own."

DePaoli has spent more than 30 years with the Navy Reserve, and was a supply chain and human resources executive with corporate purchasing turnaround experience and Lean Six Sigma deployments. Now, he is the Management Program Director at Marian University in Fond du Lac, Wis. and Principal of Apollo Solutions, a consulting firm specializing in HR, supply chain and Lean Six Sigma. He is also the author of the book Common Sense Procurement.

As DePaoli sees it, procurement professionals should be leading change within their organizations--because of all the relationships they manage. "They drive money to the bottom line," he says.

The 195-page Common Sense Supply Management

also provides all readers need to know to transform a sourcing operation including information on Lean, <u>Six Sigma and Lean</u> Six Sigma; Kaizen and performance metrics. It has chapters on global sourcing, e-procurement and p-cards, and a glossary of Lean Six Sigma and supply management terms.

The book is geared toward procurement professionals at every stage in their career. DePaoli also recommends it to his college students.

Any author that can combine "Vulcan Mind Meld" and "Coach Athletic Teams" on the same page (P.34) earns my attention. Dr. Tom DePaoli's story telling manner combines the ability to share insights and lessons in an easily digestible form while providing a relatively painless learning opportunity for the reader. Thank you Dr. Tom!

Coming from a young professional with graduate degree focus in Supply Chain, I enjoyed Dr. Tom DePaoli's writing. I found several points to be anecdotal to my real-world experiences. This made me realize the validity and value of the contents of this book and showed me how I might have better handled my situations. What was not yet applicable to my career opened my eyes and left me feeling better prepared for what the inevitable. This is a value-add read for the Supply Chain professional.

Common Sense Supply Management: Tales From The Supply Chain Trenches is a great new business book by author and business man, Dr. Tom DePaoli. Written for supply management, purchasing agents, and other management professionals, the book is full of stories, tips, and "buyers beware."

Any business professional could learn something from this book. It is a straight forward read that is enlightening and enjoyable. Highly recommended!!

Dr. Tom's uses the story teller technique in this book and I felt that it was both pertinent and enlightening. I especially enjoyed the use of baseball to build relationships in Japan. It is obvious that the author loves supply management and wants to help supply management professionals everywhere. This book is a great start if you want to transform a company.

Buyers Meeting Point Review Kelly Barner (Shrewsbury, MA United States)
This review is from: Common Sense Supply Management: Tales From The Supply Chain Trenches (Paperback)
Two years ago, we posted our review of `Common Sense Purchasing' by Dr. Tom DePaoli. In September 2012 he published a new book that reflects a broader perspective on his experience and our profession. By taking a step up - or back - however you chose to see the difference between purchasing and supply management, Dr. Tom takes a new look at the challenges and opportunities in supply management and presents them by sharing many of his own experiences as an independent management consultant.

We'll be delving further into Dr. Tom's perspective in an interview with him in February. His short segment writing format allows the reader to get through a number of mini-cases quickly in the first section of the book titled `Tales from the Supply Management Trenches'. Dr. Tom then spends the remaining chapters of the book taking on one subject at a time in greater depth. There is something for everyone, including Six Sigma, negotiation, governance, bureaucracy, and strategy. Supply management professionals will also appreciate his checklists and glossary of terms.

Looking back on Dr. Tom's time spent `in the trenches', I particularly appreciated his desire to meet a goal and then go one step further for the sake of achieving optimal performance. In one of his engagements, he was working with an integrated paper company to transform their purchasing group into a supply management operation. Using Six-sigma methodologies, they reduced workload and errors before completing a successful supplier rationalization effort. Rather than considering the transformation complete just because expectations had been met, he and his team took the additional step of putting a p-card program in place for their `super-users', eliminating nearly all paperwork.

Other themes of note include the need to have empathy for suppliers in order to establish collaborative relationships and balancing the importance of social media with the effectiveness of face-to-face communication. Technology has its place somewhere behind enabled people and process. As Dr. Tom puts it, "The procurement must come before the e".

Dr. Tom's deep experience and long career in the supply management space make this a book best related to by practitioners with some experience in the field rather than a primer for those new to the game. As to which trenches you currently find yourself in: supply chain, procurement, and purchasing professionals in any industry will benefit from Dr. Tom's experiences and honest retelling of both successes and lessons learned.

10. A Conversation with Dr. Tom DePaoli, Author of Common Sense Supply Management Buyers Meeting Point Review Kelly Barner (BMP)

This month's featured publication is Common Sense Supply Management. Since we have worked with author Dr. Tom DePaoli in the past, we took the opportunity of this new book being out to get an update on his perspective of supply management as a discipline, how social media is affecting the interactive dynamics, and on our role in the larger organization.

If you are interested in learning more about Dr. Tom's work, visit the www.apollosolutions.us website. You can also read our review of 'Common Sense Purchasing' on The Point.

Buyers Meeting Point: Do you have a working definition of 'Supply Management' in your mind? What changed in our profession or in your career that caused you to focus this book on supply management after writing Common Sense Purchasing?

Dr. Tom DePaoli: I did have a working definition of supply management when I started the book. I emphasized the relationship aspect. I somewhat <u>agree</u> with <u>the ISM definition</u>. "The identification, acquisition, <u>access</u>, positioning, management of resources and related capabilities the organization needs or potentially needs in the attainment of its strategic objectives." Supply management is much more strategic than the traditional concept of purchasing. Since I have transformed many traditional purchasing organizations into supply management organizations I understand the strategic nature of supply management. The other difference is that in supply management, the relationship building is much more complicated and at multilevels. It is not just a matrix but a multidimensional matrix of relationships! The supply management professional needs versatility and powerful relationship building skills. Their understanding of the business must be broad and well grounded. Their understanding of the many marketplaces, domestic and global, is also essential.

BMP: You give many examples of the benefits of face-to-face interactions, both with suppliers and internal stakeholders. Do you feel that supply management professionals have become too reliant on virtual communication?

Dr. T: At times I believe that they do become too reliant on virtual communication. These are great tools but nothing beats face to face interaction, supplier site visits, in person quality discussions, visiting internal stakeholders and asking for their input, and just going out in the field and asking questions and learning. In my experience, these actions yield a lot more useful data and more importantly encourage collaboration. The issue is always time management and which face to face interactions are critical.

BMP: What trends have you seen with supply management professionals making use of (or missing out on) the benefits of social media?

Dr. T: Supply management professionals need to use social media more to network, share ideas and discuss problems. There are various professional supply management organizations that have running discussions that supply management professionals can participate in and share information. One of the most valuable is asking for help on sourcing especially when you are cold sourcing a new part or service. Supply management professionals will usually give you a good honest answer on a supplier and share their supplier performance data.

BMP: You make the comment that the head of supply management must be at the vice president level (p. 50). When you combine this with the need to get Finance's sign-off on savings definitions (p. 115), do you feel that Finance is the best organization for supply management to report to, or should we be positioned on the operational side of the business?

Dr. T: Supply management should be independent of the finance organization in a company. They should report directly to the CEO. Finance should sign off on the scorecard that supply management keeps especially around savings. Many financial organizations are still using standard cost techniques instead of activity costing. As you know total cost of ownership savings include many qualitative savings that must be valued fairly. Supply Management is strongly operational; no other internal organization has a bigger impact on the bottom line. We provide the critical tools, resources, services, and parts etc. that make operations possible. Often we control or influence a very large percentage of the cost of goods sold.

11. The Point by Buyers Meeting Point. Book Review: Common Sense Supply Management Kelly Barner

Two years ago, we posted our review of 'Common Sense Purchasing' by Dr. Tom DePaoli. In September 2012 he published a new book that reflects a broader perspective on his experience and our profession. By taking a step up – or back – however you chose to see the difference between purchasing and supply management, Dr. Tom takes a new look at the challenges and opportunities in supply management and presents them by sharing many of his own experiences as an independent management consultant in 'Common Sense Supply Management'.

We'll be delving further into Dr. Tom's perspective in an interview with him in February. His short segment writing format allows the reader to get through a number of mini-cases quickly in the first section of the book titled 'Tales from the Supply Management Trenches'. Dr. Tom then spends the remaining chapters of the book taking on one subject at a time in greater depth. There is something for everyone, including Six Sigma, negotiation, governance, bureaucracy, and strategy. Supply management professionals will also appreciate his checklists and glossary of terms.

Avoiding a Supply Chain Apocalypse

Looking back on Dr. Tom's time spent 'in the trenches', I particularly appreciated his desire to meet a goal and then go one step further for the sake of achieving optimal performance. In one of his engagements, he was working with an integrated paper company to transform their purchasing group into a supply management operation. Using Six-sigma methodologies, they reduced workload and errors before completing a successful supplier rationalization effort. Rather than considering the transformation complete just because expectations had been met, he and his team took the additional step of putting a p-card program in place for their 'super-users', eliminating nearly all paperwork.

Other themes of note include the need to have empathy for suppliers in order to establish collaborative relationships and balancing the importance of social media with the effectiveness of face-to-face communication. Technology has its place somewhere behind enabled people and process. As Dr Tom puts it, "The procurement must come before the e".

Dr. Tom's deep experience and long career in the supply management space make this a book best related to by practitioners with some experience in the field rather than a primer for those new to the game. As to which trenches you currently find yourself in: supply chain, procurement, and purchasing professionals in any industry will benefit from Dr. Tom's experiences and honest retelling of both successes and lessons learned.

12. How Can We Get Young People Interested in Supply Chain Professions?

Many high school and college students are unaware of all the opportunities in the supply chain. Their concept of it tends to be warped by media stereotypes and the lack of career counselors who really understand the depth and breadth of all the possibilities and positions in the supply chain. Many students have not even considered the option of starting a career in this growing and dynamic arena.

Some recent surveys of high school seniors show a general lack of understanding of the possibilities of logistics careers. Supply chain jobs are rarely mentioned by high school counselors or even at many college level job fairs. The only active promoter of supply chain careers that I could verify was ISM or the Institute of Supply Management. So what can supply chain professionals do to encourage careers in the supply chain?

We should use similar tactics that universities and colleges now use to recruit students. This recruitment does concentrate on the Internet. Just about every potential future supply chain student has a Facebook, LinkedIn, Instagram or other internet sites. First, we should consider creating an employment brand to attract students to supply chain careers. We should use social networks to connect better with students and generate interest.

Local ISM affiliates should have parts of their websites geared to attracting students to supply chain professions. The ISM affiliates should try to build a virtual relationship with interested students. The breadth and depth of possible supply chain professions does create a challenge, but this variety should attract even more students. Of course virtual job fairs are becoming more common; so cooperation and participation from supply chain employers should be encouraged.

We cannot just stop at the Internet. Traditional tactics like tours of supply chain employers, internships, scholarships and educational seminars should also be employed. It is obvious that we have many tactics that could influence students to consider a supply chain career. The challenge will be to measure the effectiveness of these tactics. When researching this blog post, I was astounded by the lack of effort and coordination in encouraging supply chain careers. There is literally nowhere to go but up.

Finally every supply chain employee should act as an ambassador for a supply chain career and encourage young people to consider the possibility of an exciting an varied career in the supply chain. People are the most important aspect of supply chain optimization.

Dr. Tom DePaoli

4 NEGOTIATIONS

1. Mega Negotiations Story

Here is a story about a strategy we used which I called mega-negotiations. We were very lucky that all the elements fell in place and we had hungry suppliers. The size of the negotiations gave us strong leverage.

These were the ground rules we established for a $5 billion dollar bid of supplier work for major expansion of chemical plants.

1. There would be only one round of bids. We urged the suppliers to give the bid their best shot. We didn't have the time to manage multiple bids.

2. We announced that we would, in many cases, narrow down the areas where we had two preferred suppliers to one, unless we had a good business reason for keeping two.

3. Although we had negotiated some significant total-cost-of-ownership savings in the current contracts, we were open to enhancements from the suppliers and distributors.

4. We told the suppliers that we would not accept their standard spare parts packages as we had in the past. We would challenge their typical spares packages, but would be especially open to creative ways of them controlling and managing the spares at minimal or no cost to us.

5. OEMs (Original Equipment Manufacturers) could

work with distributors to propose any additional creative services to provide us.

Believe it or not we saved over $1 billion with this approach. We were stunned.

2. Purchasing Leaders Need a Combination of Exceptional One-Off Leadership Traits

Running a purchasing or supply chain organization poses unique challenges to a leader. Purchasing organizations are constantly "fighting fires", handling unique crises and influencing a broad network of people internally and externally. The range of personal contacts, cultural differences, emotions and challenges is global. In two of my books I have used poetic license and characterized the so called normal purchasing day as "zoo-ee". Although many of the skills that I discuss are also required by other leaders, the sheer nature of the purchasing beast demands a special combination of these skills.

One of the most valued characteristics of a leader is integrity. A purchasing leader needs to never waiver in being honest to everyone in all their relationships. The quickest way to demoralize your team is to not keep your word. There can be no compromise on this trait.

One of the first things a purchasing leader must make clear is what is acceptable ethical behavior. Publish and conduct classes on purchasing ethical standards. I have been fortunate to work for companies that have clear standards and strong ethics. I personally condone a zero tolerance of any gifts or gratuities including lunches or dinners from a supplier or anyone. I recommend purchasing actually budget dollars for these events and strive to not even give a semblance of any favoritism.

Because of the frenetic atmosphere; a purchasing leader must be a working leader or "hands on" resource especially when a crisis develops. Leading from the front is a requirement.

Clear goal setting and the flexibility to constantly adjust goals is a skill that must be repeatedly practiced and communicated. This goes hand in hand with the ability to provide come discipline and structure to the team in light of all the pressures and deadlines. Along with this, the talent to delegate and not to micromanage is essential. This encourages team members to take risks and grow. Purchasing leaders need to show that they truly care for their team by personally conducting training in many areas.

Curiosity and the drive to wander around and find out what is really happening, especially in other departments and with suppliers, often yields useful knowledge and actionable projects. Getting visible and being approachable cements relationship building which is the linchpin of the art of purchasing.

Sheer drive and the perseverance to not quit seizes the imagination of team members and other employees as well. I call this "indomitable spirit" and it is contagious. Below is my list of one-off purchasing leadership traits along with additional complimentary traits that develop from them. Finally never lose sight of the fact that leading by example is not working, unless your team is following and exceeding your example.

One-Off Purchasing Leadership Traits	Complimentary Leadership Traits
Integrity	Admitting mistakes
Clear goal setting	Strong and visible metrics
Relationship building	Empathy
Flexibility in priorities	Adaptability
Providing discipline and structure	Strength during crisis
Delegation skills	Trusting your employees
Training ability	Expertise
Indomitable spirit	Celebrating successes

3.   Know Your Suppliers' Industry Cold

The best piece of negotiations advice I ever received was to know the capabilities of your supplier, their industry, their competitors, their cost drivers, their margins, and their capabilities better than they do! This is time consuming, but it's a powerful tool. It requires homework, digging, and flat-out hard work. Once a supplier realizes that you understand them, it eliminates all the negotiation game playing and posturing. You will be surprised how fast they can now focus on real issues and problem solving once they know you can't be traditionally bamboozled. You obviously can't do this with every supplier only the most important and most strategic ones. It's a powerful negotiation tactic based on knowledge not histrionics. Level the playing field with your knowledge! Roll up your sleeves, dig deep, and become an industry expert. Suppliers will be impressed with your knowledge then cooperative.

4. Information-based Negotiations is a Superior Approach

Information-based negotiations are an approach to negotiations that emphasizes deep knowledge of the supplier and its industry. It varies greatly from some traditional approaches to negotiations. It's not the adversarial Win-Lose negotiation style with the emphasis on game playing, exposing untruths, and taking full advantage of the supplier's weaknesses. This old approach is a competitive winner-takes-all system that rarely builds longstanding, deep relationships with suppliers. Information-based negotiations are not based upon the Win-Win model, either. Information or knowledge is definitely power, but in information-based negotiations, the supply chain professional gains a deep knowledge of the supplier's industry, their margins, and their culture. In essence, this is a deep immersion or empathy with the supplier and their competitive landscape.

5. Information-Based Negotiations Are The Superior Option

Traditional negotiation styles are short on mutual gain and can't adapt very readily to changing market conditions or competitive situations. The information-based approach has tremendous flexibility to cope with market and industry changes. Information drives decisions—not emotions or one-upmanship. It requires the supply chain professional to become the resident expert on a market or an industry and yields much more significant long-term gains than traditional approaches.

6. There's No Glamor In An Information-Based Negotiations Approach

The information-based approach requires immense research about the industry, the supplier's financial condition, and competitive forces. Some suppliers may be very reluctant to provide financial information and their margins. The supply chain professional must work to overcome this reluctance and build trust with the supplier. Understanding their culture and their organization is critical. You are, in essence, trying your best to put yourself in their shoes and mimic, as well as possible, their anxieties and fears about the whole process. The information-based approach is not for the fainthearted or for those who do not want to persevere. It should only be exercised for critical materials or services. These are those that have a major impact on your bottom line or can give you a critical competitive advantage. One key guide would be if your customers value the aspect that the supplier brings to the table. Since it requires ongoing market research, and it works better when executives are exchanged (stay in person at the site and become part of the team) however, the resources necessary to pull off such an information-based approach should not be underestimated.

7. Mastering Information Based Negotiations Dr Tom DePaoli

An information-based negotiation is a radically

different approach to negotiations. It emphasizes deep knowledge of the supplier and their industry. It transgresses from some traditional approaches to negotiations. It is not the adversarial win-lose negotiation style with the emphasis on game playing, theatrics and taking full advantage of a supplier's weaknesses. An information-based negotiation is not the win-win model either. Information or knowledge is power, but in information-based negotiations the purchasing professional gains a deep understanding of the supplier's industry, their margins and their culture. In essence this is an immersion or empathy with the supplier and their competitive landscape. The best way to describe it is that the purchasing professional knows as much or more about the supplier and their industry as they do!

In my recent book Common Sense Supply Management I state, "The very best piece of negotiations advice I ever received was to know the capabilities of your supplier, their industry, their competitors, their cost drivers, their margins and their capabilities better than they do. It requires a lot of homework, digging and flat out work. You obviously cannot do this with every supplier only the most important and most strategic ones. It is a powerful negotiation tactic based on knowledge not histrionics. There is no glamour in the information-based approach it requires immense research about the industry, the suppliers financial condition and competitive forces. Understanding their culture and their organization is critical. You are in essence trying your best to put yourself in their shoes, and mimic as best as possible their anxieties and fears about the whole process. The information-based approach is not for the faint hearted or those who do not want to persevere. It should only be exercised for critical materials or services. It requires ongoing market research and it will work better when executives are actually exchanged with the supplier on their site. The resources and commitment to pull off such an information based approach are significant."

With the Internet the gathering of information for the information based negotiations approach has been greatly facilitated. There are numerous industry reports, websites and search engines that can help the purchasing professional. Nothing beats personal face-to-face contact and dialogue with numerous suppliers in a particular industry. They all have a fairly keen knowledge of their competitors which can rapidly improve your overall knowledge. Since many industries are oligarchic in nature, once you understand the top three or four players in the industry you have a real good foundation from which to start partnerships with your chosen supplier.

I suggest the purchasing professional consider using the Porter Five Forces analysis. Although this used extensively in marketing and marketing analysis, it can be invaluable to the purchasing professional. This will provide a good start for industry understanding. Another good source for information about suppliers and particular industries are distributors. Often they are glad to provide information about suppliers and especially their customer service. Here is a general diagram of the approach to information based negotiations that I have used:

One additional tactic I have successfully used during the initial trust building phase is to mutually do supply chain process mapping of internal processes but with a twist. The supplier comes to your site and maps your processes, then presents it to your cross functional team to check their understanding. Then the purchasing professional ventures to the supplier's site and performs a similar mapping. Often this sparks a new creative exchange of ideas. The information-based approach has tremendous flexibility to cope with market and industry changes. Information drives decisions not emotions or one-upmanship. It requires the purchasing professional to become the resident expert on a market and an industry. It yields much more significant long term gains than traditional or even win-win approaches. Using this approach is one of the best methodologies for transforming your supply chain and developing true breakthroughs with your supplier.

5 SUPPLIERS

1. Measuring Up Your Suppliers

Suppliers that have had experience with non-traditional purchasing concepts, alliances and partnerships definitely have an advantage when it comes to developing a deep relationship with them. Make sure you take the time to explain your procurement or supply chain strategy to them and to take the time to understand their strategy. They need to know what's in it for them. Make it clear and measurable. Feeling good about each other will not get to the bottom line. Appearances do count. You can size up a supplier's partner quotient a lot by actual site visits and talking to their employees at all levels. Smiling faces are better than growls and disgruntled remarks. This new frontier with suppliers has some particular characteristics. These characteristics include most favored customer contracts, elimination of incoming inspection, reduction of supplier base, early supplier involvement in design, value engineering, mutual cost reductions, targeting of non-production company costs, the complete integration of key suppliers into the business, and extensive use of cross-functional teams. This quantum leap philosophy with suppliers requires the education of purchasing personnel, rapid access to information and supplier empowerment. Cross-functional business teams and a constant dedication to improve and to reduce time to market are key elements.

Quantum leaps are usually made by actually listening to the supplier and implementing their recommendations. Rarely do they occur from internal suggestions. Suppliers are the experts on their particular parts or service not you. Heed their suggestions.

We once had a supplier recommend a simple design change on an iron casting. Not only was it cheaper but the production line was ecstatic because it was much easier to assemble. The former appendage of the old design had often broken off during assembly.

2.   Sizing up Your Suppliers and Preparing Them for Your Strategy.

Suppliers that have had experience with non-traditional purchasing concepts, alliances and partnerships definitely have an advantage when it comes to developing a deep relationship with them. Make sure you take the time to explain your procurement or supply chain strategy to them and to take the time to understand their strategy. They need to know what's in it for them. Make it clear and measurable. Feeling good about each other doesn't get to the bottom line. Appearances do count. You can size up a supplier's partner quotient a lot by actual site visits and talking to their employees at all levels. Smiling faces are better than growls and disgruntled remarks. This new frontier with suppliers has some particular characteristics. These characteristics include most favored customer contracts, elimination of incoming inspection, reduction of supplier base, early supplier involvement in design, value engineering, mutual cost reductions, targeting of non-production company costs, the complete integration of key suppliers into the business, and extensive use of cross-functional teams.

This quantum leap philosophy with suppliers requires the education of purchasing personnel, rapid access to information and supplier empowerment. Cross-functional business teams and a constant dedication to improve and to reduce time to market are key elements.

3. Just How Many Strategic Suppliers and How to Select Them.

Strategic sourcing is a disciplined process organizations implement in order to more efficiently purchase goods and services from suppliers. The goal is to reduce total acquisition cost while improving value. A Strategic sourcing strategy should be initiated immediately. A comprehensive sourcing methodology should be followed religiously to include strategic alliance and strategic relationship building with key suppliers. Key supplier alliances must be established. Supplier rationalization (reduction) must be accomplished first and dramatically. Many consulting firms offer a Strategic Sourcing Management solution that walks online users through each step of a consulting-type procurement methodology, including gathering data, analyzing requirements, and setting strategy, as well as executing e-procurement through shopping e-marketplaces, conducting reverse auctions, and using other methods that are built into the application.

Here is a Strategic Sourcing Step Process that outlines an iterative six-step process:

Assess Opportunity
Assess Internal Supply Chain

Assess Supply Markets
Develop Sourcing Strategy
    Implement Strategy
    Institutionalize Strategy

4.   Testing Suppliers Capabilities Always Do A Road Test

Never incorporate a new supplier without an actual test run of buying an item from them period and no exceptions. Have a purchasing professional pretend they are an end user, play dumb and actually order an item form the new supplier. Review the entire transaction process to include acknowledgement and invoice payment. Check on status often. This one road test tip will save you mountains of headaches and resistance to change. Folks do not really want new suppliers. They will latch on to any mistake to justify their resistance and castigate the new supplier. During trial periods new suppliers are most vulnerable to detractors and attackers. Make sure you meet frequently with them. You need to act almost with SWAT team efficiency when a problem occurs and solve it immediately. Agree to problem solving procedures in advance and deadlines. Solve glitches and explain what happened openly. This is not the time for shoving things under the rug or stonewalling problems. Fix them on the spot whenever possible.

5.   Hell Hath No Fury Like a Supplier Scorned

We once had a machine tool supplier who had lost

our bid spread the rumor that the supplier selection team was not fair in the process and that the supplier that we selected was going to go bankrupt. Fortunately we had the union president and many shop floor people on the cross-functional selection team. They were irate and worked hard to assure plant personnel that the process had been fair and held team meetings to show the work that we had done. The supplier that we had selected also gave us documents on their credit rating from our local bank. The rumor soon collapsed.

The new supplier actually provided us a PC to directly connect to them and access to their inventory. They came on site and rearranged our inventory, bar-coded it and purchased back obsolete tools. The shop floor personnel again surrendered their "bogey" or hidden inventory and developed great confidence in their service.

Often disgruntled suppliers will sow seeds of doubt especially when a new supplier is selected. Best advice is to totally ban them from your property and all further contact with the company. Purchasing should have the first and last say on which suppliers are even allowed on company property. Do not back down on this issue. Backdoor purchasing by other departments especially engineering is rampant in many companies. Nip it in the bud. Punish the "back door Bugga Lou" dancers.

6.   Reduce Suppliers First When Transforming

Radically reducing the number of suppliers is one of the first efforts that must be tackled. You can't have "relationships" with thousands of suppliers. It's difficult enough to have strong relationships with just a few key suppliers. Ruthlessness is necessary. This is not the time for compassion or backing off your supplier-reduction goals. Set the new supplier standards high. You will be surprised. Many will not want to participate under your new, higher expectations. Does the supplier add value, or is the supplier a product of misplaced loyalty? We once cut a base of five thousand suppliers to 252 in three months. It can be done, but ruthlessness was required.

7.   Supplier D-I-V-O-R-C-E Is Tough For Many

Many end-users have personal stakeholder relationships in certain suppliers and the relationships developed over the years with these suppliers. A transformation plan must be established to deal with the adjustment to new relationships with new suppliers. Use a change-management model to address these issues and guarantee the acceptance of any e-procurement initiative. Breaking up is hard to do, as the song says, but it must be done and done quickly. Many buyers cannot stay objective when dealing with a long-term supplier. Give them a chance but stay objective and open to new suppliers.

8.   Ramming the Supplier Savings Iceberg

The Iceberg of Supplier Opportunity theory holds that only five to ten percent of efficiency is gained via price, and it's the area of least resistance and work. The ninety to ninety-five percent (hidden costs) of the so-called new frontier of supplier exploration is bottom-line, total-cost-of-ownership savings of using a preferred supplier. This is the one area of the greatest resistance and opportunity. This is the realm of relationship building that requires increasing communication and the building of trust. Flexibility in supplier relationship building is a must.

9. Pick the Right Supplier Partners Or Else

Don't generate a boatload of partnerships or alliances with suppliers. True partnerships are deep relationships, and they must be tightly controlled and evaluated. It makes no sense to partner with hundreds of suppliers just for the sake of using the partnership term. True partnerships require major energy, relationship effort, money, and time. Pick them carefully and wisely.

10. Strong Supplier Expectations Work, Use Them

Here is a good example of a supplier expectation: We seek suppliers that can help us continuously improve. In order to encourage this behavior, we are willing to split hard improvement savings with you 50-50 for the first year of these savings. We need your help in educating end-users, designing manuals, working with cross-functional teams, and introducing new products. We want to take advantage of your technical expertise. We value suppliers with good technical services and those who can keep us informed of leading edge technologies that we can employ.

11. Seek Out Increased Cooperation From Suppliers. Cycle Time Can Be Reduced.

Document all supplier-driven innovations and improvements. Increase and document the number and type of direct links with suppliers, especially direct electronic ties to your production schedule and EDI. Develop in-depth alliance relationships with a few key suppliers at a strategic level to make your quantum leaps in cycle-time reduction. Then measure the success of the alliance by measuring the reduced cycle time. Also, survey your key suppliers and ask them what they think of the progress of the alliances.

6 KAIZENS

1. Kaizens Work for Marketing Plans!

I once was involved with a major transformation of a worldwide logistics organization. At the start of the transformation, they had twenty-six divisions. They had decided to reorganize and needed some basis for the reorganization. I suggested that we first do a marketing plan, which was greeted by disbelief and catcalls. I explained my strategy and said that first we had to find out what our market segments were and agree on that. We did fifty focus groups, deep marketing research and narrowed down our customer segments to six. This was a monumental voice of the customer exercise and we received a good short list of what our customers really valued.

However, the very first thing we did was do an As Is process map of where the organization was in the present state with all the reporting relationships and responsibilities. This was a long hard and complicated process but the Kaizen team discovered that there was much duplication and that 95% of the steps were not really valued by our customers. We then did a To Be process map of the future recommended state of the organization.

What we did next was again look at all twenty-six divisions and try to determine exactly what each did. We then looked at it in terms of which of the six customer segments they served the best, or were most likely to serve the best. Much to our surprise, there were no "in-between" divisions; each division fell within a particular customer segment. All of the division heads agreed with their customer segment alignment. The consensus process was really very readily accepted.

Once we presented this information to the CEO, he immediately suggested that we consolidate twenty-six divisions into six. The Kaizen team had done its homework. Obviously this Kaizen team took more time that a traditional Kaizen but the tools used were practically the same. Each division would now have a customer champion, whose main mission was to meet the needs of that particular customer segment. After much work, job analysis, and feedback from the division heads, we consolidated into six divisions. We eliminated over 600 positions, but we did avoid layoffs with attrition and by offering early retirement.

Over the years, the organization had gotten out of touch with their mission and customer base. Once the reorganization was executed, when we got our customer-service metrics, we were pleasantly surprised to see that they'd improved dramatically. Now the organization's employees could focus more on actual customers and their needs, instead of defending their organizational silos. Soon other organizations asked how we had accomplished this, and we shared our data with them.

2. Software Data Collection and Kaizen Techniques

A major purchasing software system was to be installed at a multi-national company. The software was specific to each plant or service department. Teams of consultants would visit each plant and try to gather the necessary data that the software installers need to install the software of the particular plant. That data was then given to the software installer to feed to the purchasing software system and then the system went live.

The error rate for the new plant systems was atrocious and the punch lists (errors) were huge. The client was growing increasingly skeptical about the software.

The software installers decided to have a Kaizen event. They did invite some data collectors to participate. It became blatantly obvious that there was no standard data collection process or technique that the data collectors used. Data was provided on spreadsheets, hand written papers, MS word documents etc. There was no order or structure to how the data was collected. When the software installers received the data it was almost impossible to be accurate with it.

The Kaizen leader took a bold step and asked the software installers to design the As Is process from scratch, not an easy Kaizen task but necessary. The installers noted that there were 420 different screens that data had to be entered on when the software was installed. They brainstormed what to do and came up with a plan to design an Excel spreadsheet with 420 sheets or one for each screen. Essentially each spreadsheet somewhat mimicked the entry screen with instructions about the data. The data collectors in the Kaizen not only agreed to the new As Is but sold it to the other data collectors. The spreadsheet soon became more and more sophisticated and made the data collector's job much easier by eliminating duplicate entries and creative macros.

The data entry error rate dropped from over 50% to less than 1 percent. The client's confidence in the new procurement system rose and they ordered multiple new installations.

3. Employee Orientation Shortened Via the Kaizen Way

After completing my new employee orientation at a new company that hired me, I was astounded by the redundancy and the lack of coordination of the process. Essentially employees were given a checklist and told to get signatures or initials on a laundry list of orientation items. No time limit or deadline was provided. Employees were put on their own, to go about and about, to complete the checklist. It took me two weeks to complete the employee checklist and much of the "orientation" that I received from each department on the checklist was haphazard at best.

A Kaizen team was formed which I led to look at the orientation process and recommend changes. The team actually walked the process and was astounded that the entire process walking distance was at least three miles and often the person who was supposed to "orientate" the new employee was not available. There was a high level of frustration with all new employees as they went through the process.

The team did a Voice of the Customer analysis and discovered that about 80% of the items on the checklist were not really essential and did not require the new employee to be physically present in the department indicated on the list.

In designing the As Is process, the Kaizen team made heavy use of Internet and invented a New Employee Orientation Web site. Many of the departments on the check off list already had orientation PowerPoints or webinars for new employees. All the Kaizen team had to do was organize them on the website and make sure the departments kept them up to date. In addition we provided access for new employees to work related information like phone lists, email lists, FAQs etc. that drastically reduced their anxiety and questions.

The cycle time for the orientation was reduced from two weeks down to 2-3 days or less. More importantly a much better first impression was made on the new employee.

4.   Reducing Workload via Kaizen Tools

When I took over as head of a Procurement Division there were three Plants with over $500,000,000 in purchases per year. I was to transform Purchasing into Supply Management with some Lean Six Sigma tools. Plant senior management decided to downsize my department at the plant where I was located at from eight to four, starting from day one. The plant manager was not committed to the transformation attempt and wanted it to fail. I decided to do everything in my power to not fulfill his wish.

At the first meeting I had with the department team two people started to cry. They did not know how they were going to keep up with the work. I pledged that within six months, they would have enough spare time, that they would be coming to me asking me what to do to move the business ahead. They all laughed at the statement. I volunteered to take over buying of one of the major components in the plant. I of course had no idea about the workload involved in the buying process. The next day four file drawers of paperwork for the component were moved into my office. I spent a week creating a database to help me manage the component which had no previous reliable information. Eventually a supplier helped me improve the database and ordering process.

I soon found out that purchasing data was scarce or non-existent. Purchasing employees could not give me any good summary statistics and were so caught up in firefighting that confusion reigned supreme. No one could adequately explain the purchase order process. There were no standard operating procedures. Undaunted, I actually rolled up my sleeves and typed purchase orders myself just to get an idea of what happens. We did a process map of the purchase order process. We locked to doors to the department while we had Kaizen process mapping meetings (As Is).

We all went on a data expedition and since I knew some computer programming and could query from the company databases we started to compile our data. We discovered that we had approximately 40,000 transactions or buys per year. By using a Pareto chart we saw that over 80% of the purchase orders were under $200. The vast majority of our purchases were small dollar items. Additionally only twenty people did about 90% of these buys. They were our super users or power requisitioners. We decided to concentrate on them and educate them about our efforts to transform the entire process. We designed a short order purchase form for purchases under $1000 that they could use. They participated in the design of the form. No interface with purchasing was required for the form. The middleman (purchasing) was eliminated. The only catch was they had to buy from a list of our preferred suppliers. If they wanted to deviate from the list they needed to get our approval.

We did a new process map (To Be) for the short order form with the super users participating. We created a manual and SOP for the super users with the preferred supplier list, contact information and basic purchasing terms, rules etc. We posted a process flow map in the department for everyone to see.

Our workload was drastically reduced and the buyers did not have to worry about these small purchase orders. In addition out suppliers remarked that the error rate on these short orders was greatly reduced. We recognized super users who had error free months and who worked well with suppliers. We eventually switched to purchase cards for these twenty super users which practically eliminated all paperwork.

Finally we had time for supplier rationalization or reduction and strategic initiatives. Again we mined the data and found out that we had over 20,000 suppliers. With hard work and consolidation of buys we got that number down to 209. We set up preferred suppliers and greatly simplified the entire process from requisition to payment. We standardized payment terms which greatly relieved accounts payables workload who soon became our allies.

We essentially used all the tools of the Kaizen event but not quite in the sequence order that is recommended.

In four months not six, my employees had the confidence and trust in me to come to my office and admit that they had nothing to do that day and ask what could they work on to move the business ahead. Most of this progress was due to using some simple Lean Six Sigma process improvement tools.

5. Kaizen Kreativity: Practical Excellence in the Everyday Written by Strategy Magazine

Kaizen. It's what the Japanese use to define "improvement" or a "change for the best." In business, it's a system of continuous improvement in any number of areas, to include technology, productivity, culture, and the like. Tom DePaoli, Management Program Director at Marian University in Fond du Lac Wisconsin, and CEO of Apollo Solutions, knows a thing or two about kaizen and its best practices. He found a way to share it in his newly released book, Kaizen Kreativity (Oops!):Don't Be Afraid of Looking Stupid. I'm an Expert at It.

STRATEGY: Tell us in your own words about kaizen.

DEPAOLI: The kaizen concept was originally created as part of the Toyota Production System and it's still one of the most widely-used programs in the manufacturing industry. However, it works equally well in service industries. Toyota originally created it to reduce waste and production errors. The kaizen concept has now evolved into a continuous improvement tool that looks at all aspects of a work process.

STRATEGY: What motivated you to write the book?

DEPAOLI: I wanted to share my personal experiences with the kaizen technique and my success stories. I wanted to give the readers a clear understanding of what works and what doesn't work. The kaizen can be a fun and creative way to make progress and I wanted the reader to make it enjoyable for everyone.

STRATEGY: And, who will find the most benefit from reading it?

DEPAOLI: The book is written for anyone interested in process improvement or the kaizen concept. Chapter Two, "How to Read This Book," guides both the experienced kaizen practitioner and new practitioner in a recommended approach to reading the book and using the kaizen method.

STRATEGY: What exactly happens when a kaizen event occurs?

DEPAOLI: There are over forty actual stories in the book that show which kaizen tool was used and how the tool was successful. A kaizen event requires superb organization and a dedicated team willing to change for the better. Above all, an enthusiastic sponsor is critical for success. Readers learn much more from storytelling.

STRATEGY: What about the name? What made you choose this one in particular?

DEPAOLI: I wanted people to feel comfortable in making mistakes and not to have a fear of looking stupid. We learn the most from our mistakes. I certainly have.

DePaoli explains that readers can expect to learn how to avoid the same mistakes he has made, while increasing the probability of success. "Organization of a kaizen event is critical," he says. "I hope the book gives readers a structure and the tools for a kaizen event." You can take the first step toward creating your own with the purchase of DePaoli's book. To visit his site, www.apollosolutions.us, where you can learn more and purchase Kaizen Kreativity (Oops!): Don't Be Afraid of Looking Stupid. I'm an Expert at It, click here.

6. Kaizen: Small Changes, Spectacular Results
Review by Susan Avery
MyPurchasingCenter.com

Charged with leading process improvement? Stop beating yourself up over it!

While the responsibility may seem daunting--and process change is an area where procurement must take a lead role--there is a way that can help you realize real results for your organization.

Kaizen, a philosophy of reducing waste while constantly improving the process, is one way. In fact,

91

Kaizen means change for the better.

That's thinking of Dr. Tom DePaoli, Management Program Director at Marian University in Fond du Lac, Wis. DePaoli, also the CEO at business consulting firm Apollo Solutions, is the author of the new book Kaizen Kreativity (Oops!)--Don't Be Afraid of Looking Stupid. I'm an Expert at It.

"What happens a lot of time with process improvement is that consultants are very dogmatic with their methodology," he tells My Purchasing Center. "People are intimidated. I try to make it fun and I encourage people to be creative."

DePaoli's book, Kaizen Kreativity, is a fundamental field manual or guide, in which he simplifies the methodology for the reader, shares success stories, and points out mistakes he's made using Kaizen. He wrote the book for both novice and experienced users.

In it, he writes, "the book is a summary of many of the Kaizen lessons that I learned in my career...I have woven together many of the lessons learned to help you avoid the numerous mistakes that I have made....I strongly believe in the Kaizen process."

DePaoli reinterprets the definition of Kaizen for the reader as "a creative but structured approach to improve a process or to eliminate anything of non-value, by the people who actually do the work.

That's important to him. "I want to give everyone a broader perspective of process improvement," he says. "The people who benefit the most are those who are actually doing the work. That's because they understand the process. Kaizen is going to make it better for them and, ultimately, for the customer, which is important."

Avoiding a Supply Chain Apocalypse

DePaoli says Kaizen can be used by large and small companies for such projects as high operating costs, low yield rate, long cycle time and unpredictable quality.

He firmly believes that procurement should take the lead on process improvement and has written about the topic in his blog at My Purchasing Center. Not only is procurement a master at managing relationships, but also "there are only two departments that generate revenue for a company--sales and procurement. Why wouldn't procurement try to improve processes and generate more revenue?"

DePaoli shares a story of when he was working as head of procurement for company with an annual spend of $500 million and he was asked to take the organization from tactical to strategic. The company reduced head count from eight to four buyers and the plant manager was not committed to the transformation. Spend data was scarce and procurement spent much of its time "fighting fires." No one could explain the PO process.

He mapped the process and designed a new PO form for the plant's "power" requisitioners. He took procurement out of the process and mandated requisitioners purchase from preferred suppliers. He created a new process map, manual and SOP for the power requisitioners. All this, DePaoli relates in the book, drastically reduced procurement's workload, the supplier base and error rates. Eventually, the organization began using p-cards for these purchases. Soon procurement started asking to work on more strategic initiatives.

In this case, he was creative with Kaizen. "We essentially used all the tools, but not quite in the sequence recommended."

DePaoli also shares mistakes he's seen. A big one is having a sponsor who is not committed to Kaizen. "I've seen organizations build a team that's raring to go, but the sponsor drags his feet on implementation. Imagine what that does to credibility and morale."

Another is that some people proceed without a full understanding of the tools. "It's difficult to teach and examine the process at the same time," DePaoli says. "I like to teach the tools before I do the Kaizen." He also likes to use common experiences in his teaching to make his point.

In addition to the success stories and common mistakes, the 167-page book contains training exercises as well as a training presentation, a roadmap, tips, a glossary of terms and lots more.

7. In a Kaizen Always Walk the Process

If possible, the kaizen leader and all team members should actually walk the process or simulate it. The purpose is to gather information for the next step, or the as-is, current-state process flow. Often, the process may have to be walked more than once and verified. Do not skip this step ever. For a service or transaction process, you'll find that prototypes of the actual forms or emails used in the process make great props!

8. Some Suggested Kaizen Ground Rules

Here are the ground rules that I used in my Kaizens:

Team is 100% committed. No interruptions. Stick to an agenda. Use a "Parking Lot". An open mind is the key to change. Positive attitudes are essential. Resolve all disagreements. No one is to blame. Practice mutual trust and respect. One person has one vote. Everyone is equal; no position or rank. No such thing as a dumb question.

9. Preparation Before the Kaizen Is Crucial

Two to four weeks of hard preparation work by the Green Belt or Black Belt and team or kaizen leader is required for a kaizen. The kaizen leader should be a Green Belt or Black Belt. Essentially the first six kaizen tools (there are eleven) are completed or very nearly roughed out before the kaizen event. The champion (the sponsor who wants the kaizen done) and kaizen leader must identify necessary subject-matter experts (team members) required for the kaizen. The champion and kaizen leader should author a draft kaizen charter. Hold initial planning meetings with affected stakeholders to communicate the kaizen's schedule, metrics, targets, and Lean tools to be applied. Most kaizen teams hold three-to-five working meetings before the actual kaizen event.

10. Bold New Business Advice Book Tells Management and Staff: "Don't Be Afraid of Looking Stupid!" Marketing Release

From expert business consultant Dr. Tom DePaoli, 'Kaizen Kreativity (Oops!)' is an imaginative and compelling guide to an entirely new approach to improving work design and work processes. With

decades of experience in the field, Dr. DePaoli offers a
fresh look at the Kaizen method and an entertaining
willingness to stumble and get right back up again.
Dr. Tom DePaoli isn't afraid of looking stupid, and as he
tells other business leaders – "you shouldn't be afraid of
it either!"
In his new advice book, 'Kaizen Kreativity (Oops!)', Dr.
DePaoli outlines an unorthodox but effective way of
using Kaizen tools to further improvement and make
significant gains.
'Kaizen' is Japanese for "improvement" or "change for
the best" and refers to the philosophy or practices that
focus upon continuous improvement of processes in
business management. (Source: Dictionary). A tried-and-
true business philosophy, Kaizen can nonetheless be
intimidating to business executives or workers, who may
feel self-conscious or silly while participating in Kaizen
events. Dr. DePaoli's book is the first of its kind to
address these concerns and encourage participants to
shed their reserve and get the most out of the training
exercises.
Synopsis:

In his new fun and creative book Kaizen
Kreativity (Oops) or Don't Be Afraid of Looking Stupid.
I'm an Expert at It! author Dr. Tom DePaoli offers an
entertaining and creative approach to improving work
design and work processes.

Dr. DePaoli uses a variety of techniques
including storytelling, imaginative training exercises and
ready to go outlines of PowerPoints on Kaizens. Dr.
DePaoli uses self-deprecating humor to recall the many
times when he stumbled, when trying to implement

Kaizen events. The reader can gain much from these lessons. The book also serves as a good desktop guide to Kaizens with a wealth of information on how to organize for Kaizen events. This is not a dogmatic book that insists on a rigid methodology for Kaizens. Dr. DePaoli often shows that just using a few Kaizen tools can often result in significant gains.

The book will help both the novice and the experienced Kaizen leader. He uses real life examples of Kaizen tools to show how work groups can make great gains. By following these stories the reader can gain a career's worth of experience in Kaizen events. Dr. DePaoli's lessons are practical, to the point and enjoyable. Like many good business leaders, the author places getting the trust of the Kaizen work team first and foremost in his book. He emphasizes the intense preparations for the Kaizen event and overcoming the fear of asking stupid questions and conquering any trepidation of looking foolish. His book advances to tackle common mistakes in the Kaizen event, dealing with Kaizen team bad actors and building a strong relationship with the Kaizen champion. He provides an excellent workbook outline for a Kaizen event along with a strong glossary of Kaizen terms. The book provides solid elements of a desktop guide for conducting a Kaizen along with suggestions on how to make the Kaizen tools exciting. Dr. DePaoli asserts, "Above all don't be afraid of looking stupid! I'm an expert at it! And it has served me very well."

To Dr. DePaoli, recognizing imperfections or flaws are an essential part of the Kaizen process.

"I tell participants constantly – lose your fears," says the author. "Often, people are frightened of knowing what their weaknesses are in a business environment, but how else can they improve? They may be afraid of looking stupid, but that impedes progress – and only when they truly open themselves up to the experience can change happen."

Continuing: "Kaizen events are never going to go perfectly, but that's the beauty of it. In those moments when we stumble – that's when we realize our true potential. If you get up again and make a joke, or learn from it – that's when you prove your worth to the team and to the company."

'Kaizen Kreativity (Oops!): Don't Be Afraid of Looking Stupid. I'm an Expert at It' is available now in both paperback and Kindle

11. Kaizen Kreativity (OOPS!) Review by Kelly Barner at Buyers Meeting Point

Don't be Afraid of Looking Stupid. I'm an Expert at It.

Kaizen Kreativity is the fifth book by Dr. Tom DePaoli, and the third one I have reviewed. Like his other books, Kaizen Kreativity combines examples from his diverse professional past with easy to comprehend definitions and background. His lack of pretention is particularly appreciated since he often relates cases about Lean and Six Sigma. For anyone without experience using these methodologies, the terminology can be off-putting at best, and in the worst case scenario may deter people from realizing their benefits altogether.

A Kaizen, literally translated from the Japanese as "improvement" or "change for the best", is a process for carrying out Lean process improvements. As Dr. Tom states in the book, "A Kaizen is an intensive, short-term activity designed to identify and eliminate waste (p. 93). The Kaizen is an outcome of an evaluation of an inefficient process. […] Kaizens are action oriented in nature and typically one- to three-day events. The end goal is aimed at validating, evaluating, improving, and then moving from the current state map (As-Is) of the process steps selected, to implementation of the new and improved future state map (To-Be) at the completion of the event (p. 6)." http://en.wikipedia.org/wiki/Kaizen

Although they are best known in manufacturing, Kaizens offer tremendous benefits for procurement organizations. In fact, if well executed, they may result in something that looks remarkably similar to a procurement transformation. The need for a Kaizen starts with the recognition of a specific cost or process oriented problem. Examples include high quality costs, repetitive efforts, and manual processes. Kaizens are leveraged in situations when the problem is severe, as this motivates the organization and the specific individuals involved to embrace change quickly.

For organizations trying to streamline their procure-to-pay processes, the emphasis on efficiency over bureaucracy will be particularly relevant. In such cases, the future state or To-Be, ensures that the processes and guidelines put in place reduce the need for individual approvals for the majority of transactions. Kaizens also recognize and incorporate the Voice of the Customer (VOC) as one of eleven steps. If you are not a Black or Green Belt (hint: they are the two of the highest levels of certification), no need to worry. *Kaizen Kreativity* provides enough background and templates to get started, although working with someone who has the appropriate experience never hurts.

Chapter 16 addresses Kaizen Team Skills, and the three brief pages will improve the project management skills of any professional in any discipline. In his introduction, Dr. Tom warns of humorous sections, and whether he intended it or not, the section on traditional objections is like a list of 'oldies but goodies'. Here are a few of my favorites, feel free to sing along if you know the words…

"We are different from everyone else."
"You do not understand our process."
"Our processes are too complex."
"Our work is not repetitive."
"Our customers are too demanding."
Sing it again, Dr. Tom.

If you aren't yet convinced that *Kaizen Kreativity* is a worthy read, maybe you are too different from everyone else or I just do not understand your process. If you are ready to take the first step towards improved efficiency and results, *Kaizen Kreativity* and the rest of Dr. Tom's books are available on Amazon.com. You can also follow him on Twitter @DrTomDePaoli or learn more at CommonSensePurchasing.com.

12. Kaizen Book Promo Wins Over Readers

In his new fun and creative book Kaizen Kreativity (Oops) or Don't Be Afraid of Looking Stupid. I'm an Expert at It! author Dr. Tom DePaoli offers an entertaining and creative approach to improving work design and work processes. Dr. DePaoli uses a variety of techniques including story-telling, imaginative training exercises and ready to go outlines of PowerPoints on Kaizens. Dr. DePaoli uses self-deprecating humor to recall the many times when he stumbled, when trying to implement Kaizen events. The reader can gain much from these lessons. The book also serves as a good desktop guide to Kaizens with a wealth of information on how to organize for Kaizen events. This is not a dogmatic book that insists on a rigid methodology for Kaizens. Dr. DePaoli often shows that just using a few Kaizen tools can often result in significant gains. The book will help both the novice and the experienced Kaizen leader.

He uses real life examples of Kaizen tools to show how work groups can make great gains. By following these stories the reader can gain a career's worth of experience in Kaizen events. Dr. DePaoli's lessons are practical, to the point and enjoyable. Like many good business leaders, the author places getting the trust of the Kaizen work team first and foremost in his book. He emphasizes the intense preparations for the Kaizen event and overcoming the fear of asking stupid questions and conquering any trepidation of looking foolish.

His book advances to tackle common mistakes in the Kaizen event, dealing with Kaizen team bad actors and building a strong relationship with the Kaizen champion. He provides an excellent workbook outline for a Kaizen event along with a strong glossary of

Kaizen terms. The book provides solid elements of a desktop guide for conducting a Kaizen along with suggestions on how to make the Kaizen tools exciting. This is novel indispensable guide to a Kaizen event.

Dr. DePaoli asserts, "Above all don't be afraid of looking stupid! I'm an expert at it! And it has served me very well."

7 SOURCING

1.   How to Avoid Dragging Out the RFP Process

Always set a final deadline for returning an RFI or RFP. If a supplier does not meet the deadline don't consider them. Don't ever compromise a bid or the bid process by favoring certain suppliers. Many folks want to procrastinate bids. The real reason is their stake in a relationship with their homey supplier is threatened. They feel that they may be proven dead wrong especially if their favorite son supplier falters. If suppliers can't follow basic instructions on RFPs do you really want them in a relationship? I think not.

2.   Standardize Equipment and Services.

Engineers always have their pets and biases. We all do. It is critical to get them on cross functional teams to standardize parts and equipment. A goal of 80% standardized parts is realistic in many industries. Difference in brands (suppliers), OEMs, and parts must have significant added value to be justified. Try to measure quality with an obscure balkanization of OEMs and different parts (ha). Good luck. The same holds for services. Standardize them. One of the guiding principles of industrialization is standardization. Don't lose sight of it! Pursue it. Standardize whenever possible.

3.   Why Culture Can Make or Break the Global Sourcing Process

If you decide to deal directly with the source or

supplier in another country, you need to realize that reaching a strong cultural understanding will make or break the process. The task of understanding the culture of the sourcing country is the most difficult of the entire process. Culture includes social organization, political beliefs, the legal system, religious beliefs, language, and the educational system, to name just a few. Any one of these areas requires extensive study and understanding in order to be successful. It is no small task.

4. The Complexities of Global Sourcing

It's impossible to cover all the differences and complexities for every country. Some of them include currency issues, political stability, infrastructure issues, contract-law differences, high logistics costs, protectionism, and lack of managerial talent. However, there are methodologies available to help you at least have a checklist for such a global-sourcing challenge. Make sure you do a current "as-is" of your supply chain and a future "to-be." It's critical to develop delivered or all in costs.

5. Office Supplies Best Practices and Dense-Pack Sourcing

Best practices for Office Supplies are many and varied. They greatly depend on what the customer wants or the Voice of the Customer (VOC). Once I was tasked with completing an office-supplies sourcing search for a client in a major western state city at their headquarters, which housed approximately 5,000 employees downtown. I had much previous experience completing four strategic sources of office supplies, so I had a fairly good idea of the competency of the suppliers and their pricing structures. I knew which additional total-cost-of-ownership practices to ask for, such as desktop delivery, consolidated billing, and electronic catalogues. It was an exceptional situation for a supplier, because it was one delivery spot for major sales volume. Composing the request for a quote was straightforward, and I used many of the requirements that I had previously used in sourcing requests. My client was eager to get the sourcing process underway and completed quickly.

However, I soon discovered that there were three other large companies in the same city block housing an additional 15, 000 employees (20,000 total). I saw an opportunity to pool our volumes and presented a proposal to my client. I had shared our expected price reduction and other savings with them prior to the engagement. Now I proposed to the client to construct a request for quote for all of us for office supplies, thus providing even more leverage. I named it the *"dense-pack"* approach because, once again, the winning supplier would have concentrated deliveries in a close area, which would significantly reduce the winning supplier's transportation costs. The purchasing managers were skeptical at first, but luckily none of the other companies were direct competitors.

The hardest part of this approach was next: convincing the other three companies of the merits of this approach. I recommended that they each set up steering committees to choose what services they desired. We sort of used a cafeteria approach where each company selected the service they desired. Fortunately, all of them were familiar with supply management and strategic sourcing. I had to show the expected savings and get them to agree to at least some common total-cost-of-ownership reduction items. Gathering the usage data was another challenge, but we believed that we had fairly accurate volume data when we went out with the request for a quote. Getting agreement to go with the winning quote was not as difficult as I had anticipated, and all four companies had two representatives on the sourcing team. Each company agreed to select their specific supplier services that they valued and asked the suppliers to demonstrate their capability and client references.

The results were fairly astounding, and we doubled the expected price savings. The winning supplier then offered a cafeteria menu of total-cost-of-ownership savings and enhancements that each customer could select. In addition most of the companies "piggybacked" with the office supplies supplier on other services like document management (copiers), personal computer supplies etc. It also led to standardization of the office supplies used which further reduced prices.

In summary, we clearly understood the market, the pricing structure and the services offered. The biggest challenge, as usual, was getting customer buy-in and consensus.

6.   Sourcing with Cross-Functional Teams Challenges Leadership Skills

Cross-functional teams work well for the sourcing of indirect goods and services, but they require good discipline and creativity on the part of the purchasing leader of the team.

Often, the purchasing team leader must spend more time on team building and training than the actual sourcing process! This poses challenges for the purchasing team leader, but it must be done to ensure success.

Who is selected to be on the team is critical, and team members should be stakeholders with a strong degree of commitment to the outcome. The purchasing leader needs to take the time to educate and train the team on the sourcing process and internal purchasing procedures. Sometimes team members have axes to grind or prior war stories about suppliers. Their supplier biases must be dealt with before the process starts.

Start with training the team on internal value stream analysis of the indirect goods or services, basic industry information, preliminary total cost of ownership (TCO), supplier metrics and scorecard, and the disciplined steps in the sourcing process.

Get everyone involved in some task, research or small project, and have them present it to the team. Then achieve strong buy-in on the proposed sourcing criteria metrics from the entire team. In the indirect goods and services area, on time delivery, is often the most important criteria.

Frequently teams want to rush into the sourcing process without adequate background training. Pressure builds to skip so-called unnecessary steps in the sourcing process and get it over with. "We know that already" usually means "We think we know it, but don't want to do the hard homework on it!" Based on my years of experience in sourcing, skipping a step is a recipe for disaster and almost always picks the exact wrong supplier!

The purchasing leader should get the team's creative juices going. Make sure the team completely understands how the goods or services are used and actually "walk the process" of the internal supply chain and the administrative burden. In other words, track exactly what happens in every step of the internal supply chain and use any data that you have to reinforce the team's understanding. Get the benchmarking information that you can. Face the fact that for many indirect goods or services, you're paying customers have no interest in how you source them, or care about them, because this is just not critical to them. However, we know that "indirects" can have a strong negative administrative burden impact on you!

Another creative approach is to test the potential new supplier's relationship and soft skills. Invite them in for interviews and insist that your potential new supplier's representative come in and discuss their goals, experiences and past successes. A behavior-based interview is a good approach that I have used. Call up fellow purchasing managers (non-competitors recommended) who have them for a supplier, and ask about their performance and response time in a crisis. Ask point blank if the supplier has done any improvements or cost saving projects.

Finally make sure you visit the finalist supplier's sites and have them explain their own internal supply chain for the indirect goods. When the supplier is selected do not neglect to have a kickoff. Following these guidelines will help you select the best of the best suppliers for indirect goods and services.

8 STORYTELLING

1. Use Storyboards in Purchasing

Market Your Purchasing Successes with the Use of Storyboards

Purchasing professionals need to realize that they must not only market their purchasing strategies but their successes. Many purchasing professionals neglect to create a marketing plan for their organization. I use the term marketing plan synonymously with communication plan.

Some of the goals and techniques of your marketing-communication plan should be to educate top management on your strategic plans, publish results of supplier performance and surveys, publish internal customer survey results, educate personnel on purchasing and supply chain principles, emails, hold roundtables, hold town meetings, use social media, utilize newsletters, use a supply chain specific web pages, monthly letters, and announcement of successes.

Storyboards are a great way to market your successes. Storyboards require you to be disciplined in your message and fully understand your results and assertions. You must limit your words and concentrate on the essentials. Thus you must communicate explicitly and right to the point for your audience. You need to strip away the technical argot and make sure the audience can easily grasp what you have accomplished, even with a very limited knowledge of purchasing. Storyboards should adhere to a lean principle of visibility. Storyboards must be understood quickly with the maximum use of graphics, not words, spreadsheets or numbers. This is not an easy task, as a consultant we would often spent hours and days trying to accomplish this with a storyboard. Obviously purchasing often does not have the talent (full time illustrator) or resources to do this meticulously, but this is intended to be a guide.

There is no one catch all formula or template for storyboards. Often how you employ them and your particular style depends on the culture and communication norms of your organization. The important aspect is to make sure that you communicate your successes in a manner that can be readily understood by both purchasing and non-purchasing personnel. Think of storyboards as intelligent commercials that must be brief, easily remembered and upbeat.

I have provided an example of a storyboard that we used to communicate a purchase order success story. The organization that it was used in was very heavily into Lean Six Sigma, Kaizens and the DMAIC methodology (Define-Measure-Analyze-Improve-Control). We used this familiar DMAIC format to help people understand and follow what we did. It still has too many words and numbers but we needed to insure people realized the scope of what we had accomplished. The storyboard was well received and readily understood by employees. I highly recommend purchasing and supply chain professionals consider using storyboards to communicate your successes.

3. Use the Storytelling Method to Train Supply Chain Professionals

One of the oldest methods of passing down knowledge was by oral storytelling. Usually an ancient sage would be the keeper of the stories and pass them down to other tribe members. I highly recommend this method for supply chain professionals.

Here are some advantages of storytelling:

- The brain stores information by stories.
- Stories are humanizing and stimulate creativity.
- Storytelling improves listening skills.
- Storytelling builds a team culture.
- It encourages collaboration.

First, creating the right atmosphere and teamwork is essential in order to establish the validity of this method. The trust of all members of the team and non-attribution is essential. The leader of the team should leadoff and share personal supply chain stories of success and failures. There should be a general framework for the stories. In our framework, we structured the stories to first give a background of the situation or issue, then tell how resources were gathered to address the issue (approach), and finally reveal the results. Often the approach to solving the problem is more important that the actual results. Colleagues would be encouraged to ask questions and to suggest more appropriate approaches. Supply chain professionals have many touch points or people involved throughout the supply chain. Stories should not be limited to paying customers but include suppliers, colleagues, competition, other departments etc.

Here is an example:

Background: We went through comprehensive sourcing selection process with a cross-functional team. We involved all the key stakeholders and were very meticulous in our research and selection. We were highly confident that we had selected the right water pump supplier and were expecting significant hard and soft savings. The supplier had prior experience with partnerships and alliances.

Approach: Much to my surprise after two weeks I discovered that the process was not going well. Maintenance personnel were complaining about the new supplier so I decided to investigate. I walked around the plant and talked to maintenance personnel and their department heads. I soon discovered that the issue was not the quality of the pumps. The issue was the representative that the supplier had assigned to our account. The rep just could not adjust to our people or culture. The personality was not a fit.

Results: I approached the supplier and requested that a new representative be assigned to out plant. The new representative got along well with everyone and we made great progress in savings and innovation. The lesson that I learned, is that the selection team should interview the potential supplier's representative during the selection process and insure that they are a fit. We thus added "chemistry" to our selection process.

We used this same storytelling method after every sourcing event and continued to discover issues that we had missed. We then added them to our overall sourcing methodology or checklist. Storytelling is a powerful collaborative learning tool, I recommend taking full advantage of it.

9 PLANNING

1. Long Term Strategic Plan

Over 95% of purchasing or supply management organizations do not have a long-term strategic plan. This is not surprising given the dynamic and hectic pace of purchasing organizations. Many of the plans that are completed are done once, and put in a three ring binder or a hard drive to never be referenced again. These plans do require a lot of effort and support from top management to become useful and meaningful. They are essential to keeping purchasing on track and focused on the most important supply chain improvement efforts. Long-term plans serve as a great focal point for purchasing and insure that constant firefighting and other upsets do not overwhelm their efforts. They can serve as guides for the stages of organizational transformation that a purchasing department wants to achieve, and reveal to non-purchasing personnel, purchasing's long-range direction. First off, create a vision and mission statement that aligns with the organization's vision and mission statement. Be bold and make sure people realize that you are aiming for supply management not traditional bureaucratic purchasing. Try to gain a broad consensus and gather input from surveys, one-on-one meetings, research and as many employees, suppliers and customers as possible.

There are limitations to this guide. I am certain that I have missed some areas but I have tried to be as comprehensive as possible. Use this document as a guide and checklist not a dogmatic methodology. It is extremely difficult to predict the future as technology and the macro environment are rapidly changing. Global events can radically alter the supply chain and require new innovative strategies. Collaboration is the norm now, but collaboration can also be cyclical and have peaks and valleys of cooperation. People are the strength of an organization and any strategic plan that does not focus on people development is woefully inadequate. Many companies also have to cope with dealing with multi-generational group differences.

New products can require new supply chain tactics and alter your product mix landscape. Competitive pressures can often dictate rapid responses and major changes in product marketing and sourcing. Communication is becoming even more critical in this rapid paced world. The selling or marketing of the strategic plan is even more crucial.

Once in place, a strategic plan is much easier to update, review and fine tune. It is important to keep it dynamic, up to date and a living document. I hope this guide motivates the reader to take the journey of completing a strategic plan. Good luck in the journey!

2. Strategy Always Trumps Technology
The Institute for Supply Management notes that 95 percent of supply chain departments do not have a procurement strategy or long-term supply management plan. Of the 5 percent that do in fact have a strategy, only half have successfully aligned the strategy with overall business strategy. Don't be afraid to put non-traditional

metrics in your plan. Remember, people behave according to the way that they are rewarded. After you have a strategy, you must educate other employees on its tenets and the reason behind it. Get a plan and be better that the other 95%.

3. Purchasing and supply management need a five year plan. Create it.

Create a five-year strategic plan for purchasing and integrate it into the company's overall strategic plan. Get out into the field with sales and marketing to find out what the final customer really wants in your product, and get the materials and services to meet these needs. Keep track of the number of final customer contacts and the number of changes made because of their input.

10 PROCESS IMPROVEMENT

1. Purchase Orders Eliminated by Kaizen Tools

I once worked for a company with a seven-part purchase-order form, and every single purchase order had to be approved by the vice president of finance. People were so disheartened by the abysmal speed of the system that maverick ways of purchasing were rampant.

A small purchasing Kaizen team completed seven As Is process maps for each method. It was a very disheartening process fraught with delays and contradictions.

Instead of trying to make the existing processes better, we decided to start from scratch on the To Be process. Fortunately we had plenty of best practices and their process maps available for purchase orders.

We initially went to a two-part short-order form for everything under $500, and eventually to purchase cards. We eliminated ten file cabinets of forms. People soon had the confidence in the systems, and they were much more truthful in expressing their needs. The vice president of finance had more time to get IPO funding and improve our financial viability rather than spending his time deciding who should be purchasing pens and pencils.

Some tools of the Kaizen process eliminated very bureaucratic methods.

2. Storerooms and Listening to Customers (VOC)

One of the first supply chain projects that we did at a large chemical company in Alabama which involved frequently used MRO parts by the maintenance folks. First we did an As Is process map! Highly paid maintenance personnel ($30 per hour) were driving in pickup trucks, in pairs, to go to a central storeroom to pick up basic and frequently-used parts. The time lost was enormous. The feedback we got from the maintenance personnel (VOC) was that they did not trust the current system at all. We were a chemical company, and our expertise or core competency was not in storeroom, or MRO parts management. We started a supplier search for distributors with expertise in management parts and storerooms. We decided to basically outsource the management of these frequently used parts to the distributor. They examined our storeroom data, provided us software, and soon discovered the one hundred parts most-frequently used by our maintenance folks.

In other words the distributor did the To Be process map for us! Since they had strong credibility the Kaizen team formed. They then set up many free-issue or mini-storerooms throughout the large chemical plant's grounds. Our maintenance folks traveled or walked to these areas to get the parts they needed. The distributor maintained and restocked the areas. The distances were much shorter and conveniently decentralized. The maintenance people set up a steering committee (another best practice) with the distributor to review parts usage and add or subtract parts to the mini-storerooms. In Kaizen terminology this was To Be metrics! The process was greatly simplified, and the maintenance people soon developed a high degree of confidence in the distributor and the streamlined system. Then the distributor offered to reorganize our storeroom and barcode all the parts at no charge. We quickly agreed.

In another month, a shocking development occurred. We were not sure how to quantify the savings from this project and were worried that many people would not appreciate the soft savings. As stated above, many of our maintenance people had no confidence in our current storeroom system. We publicized a return-any extra-parts-with-no-questions-asked week. This was run much like a fine-free day at your local library. Our maintenance people returned over $2 million-worth of bogey or just-in-case inventory that they had been squirreling away in their toolboxes and other areas. They'd done this because they'd had zero confidence in the old system. Our new supplier accepted the parts back and gave us a large credit for the returned parts that were still usable. The distributor kept us abreast of any new storeroom-management techniques and technologies, including the RFID (Radio Frequency Identification Device). We developed a long and lasting relationship with them which became the model for our other chemical plants.

By just using a few tools of the Kaizen methodology we experienced a huge success!

3. Suggested Sample Ground Rules for Meeting Operation

Each committee should develop/review a list of ground rules at the beginning of each year. The list below provides sample ground rules that various committees have used. Your committee may wish to incorporate some of these or develop new ones.

- Start / end our meetings on time
- Come to meetings prepared.
- Stay on task; no side conversations
- Listen to others and don't interrupt.
- Follow an agenda
- Operate on consensus – seek general agreements all can "live with."
- Make decisions based on clear information.
- Bring closure to decisions
- Identify actions that result from decisions
- Members support committee recommendations
- Agree on what information goes "out" and what stays in the group.
- Accept the fact that there will be differences of opinion.
- Show mutual respect
- We will honor brainstorming without being attached to our own viewpoint.
- We will keep our own notes of the meetings
- Use Meeting Summaries (Includes Agenda Items & Minutes)
- Check egos at the door.
- Attack the problem, not the person- "no blame game"

- Share time so that all can participate
- People will speak when recognized.
- Be free to speak minds without fear of reprisal.
- Don't attribute ideas to individuals.
- Identify pending issues and agreements at end of meeting
- Raise hands (when not in a brain storming session).
- Stay on subject.

- Be concise. Do not repeat what others have said.
- Be respectful and polite.
- Raise Hands - Stay in Order except for: point of clarification or point of process
- Don't Interrupt Speaker
- Stay on Subject
- Be Concise, Don't Repeat Others
- Be Respectful, Be Polite.
- Everyone participates
- Start and finish on time
- One conversation at a time
- Silence is agreement
- Different opinions are welcome
- Challenge ideas, not individuals
- Disagree in private; unite in public
- Do what you say you'll do
- Treat everyone with courtesy and respect
- Listen actively- respect others when they are talking

- Listen to others with an open mind
- One person speaks at a time- no cross talk
- Be aware of your own and other's participation- step up and step back!
- Share your own experiences and opinions with "I" statements, rather than generalizing with "We" or "They" comments
- Respectfully challenge an idea, not a person
- Respect the groups' time and keep comments brief and to the point

4.   Procurement Needs to Lead Process Improvement Transformation

Often companies make the grievous mistake of not letting procurement select or source the consultant or consulting group to lead process improvement. Lean Six Sigma and Lean are too important to leave in the hands of other departments not familiar with the comprehensive evaluation of a bid or a proposal. In fact, procurement or supply management not only should lead the selection, but lead the entire process improvement transformation. Nothing can have more financial gain for a company than improvements in the supply chain! Here are some hard learned selection lessons.

Experience trumps everything in selecting a Lean Six Sigma or Lean consultant. It's critical that the consultant you hire has multiple experiences with multiple projects. Verification by checking with former clients is essential. Beware of consultants who want to charge exorbitant fees for all the process improvement training belt classes. You can quickly master this training internally for employees to become at least an entry level Green Belt by using the train-the-trainer concept. Belt certifications differ from company to company. Insist on training effectiveness data from the consultant and examples of successful projects and tools used in their methodology. There are hundreds of improvement tools that could possibly be used in the process improvement. There are however only about 30-40 that are used most frequently and are the most effective.

Strongly consider a fixed hourly rate especially for training, but remember that you get what you pay for. Make sure you can retain all the training materials developed during the process. Many of the available training materials are generic, and you will want to retain any customized ones for your company. Make sure the consultant understands that you will demand process improvement self-sufficiency in two years or sooner.

The consultant's people skills must be superb. Initially many members of a process improvement team are hostile to the process and transformation until they understand it. Strive to make the contract performance-based on the savings of the projects rather than amount of training delivered or other parameters that they suggest. Consider jointly developing online training courses that can be used with much greater flexibility. Process improvement meeting organization and facilitation skills are indispensable. Insist on sitting in on a live meeting that the consultant conducts like a kaizen. Observing a consultant in action is one of the best ways to judge their skills. Make sure the consultant can fit into your organization's culture and adapt to your organization's standards and norms. Nothing destroys process improvement initiatives faster than cultural mismatches.

Finally prepare your organization for the process improvement transformation. The most successful proven way to make process improvement initiatives work is to make employees accountable for it. In other words tie their cooperation, progress and training in process improvement *directly to their pay or raises.* You must financially incentivize it for them. Other so-called persuasive or cooperative approaches have a much higher failure rate.

5. Pilots Are For Doubters, Naysayers, and Obstructionists

New process or new initiative pilots are good for certain supply management ventures but don't procrastinate or extend them out ad infinitum. It's a good way for the resistance to kill you off. The burden of proof is 51 percent or reasonable. It's not beyond a reasonable doubt or a 12-0 unanimous jury vote. If you use the later criteria you will never have a successful pilot. Make sure one person is accountable for the pilot beachhead and can understand the total picture. Folks love experiments, but remember that the first rule of experiments is to have controls! If you get consensus in a kaizen, change the process, change it right away! Do not lose momentum.

6. Some Tips for Process-Improvement Meetings

The most common and most egregious mistake that the various process-improvement team leaders make is not having a meeting agenda. The agenda must be published before the meeting and distributed to team members. Team members need to anticipate what to expect in the meeting and what the intended results are—by this, I mean the deliverables. Minutes of each meeting must be taken and published before the next meeting. Minutes must be approved and/or corrected at each subsequent meeting. Always try to have a facilitator and a person taking minutes.

Maximize the visibility in the meeting; make sure all process maps are visible to everyone. Insist that team members get at least introductory training in the methodology. Trying to train team members on process-improvement tools at the same time that you're trying to improve the process is very difficult. If meetings last more than two hours, the leader is not organized, and the members won't be able to function very well.

Always set a goal of finishing at least two deliverables or milestones for each meeting, and push to have them get completed. End the meeting with asking the members what went right and what went wrong.

7. Selecting a Lean Six Sigma Consultant

Experience trumps everything in selecting a Lean Six Sigma consultant. It's critical that the consultant you hire has multiple experiences with multiple projects. Beware of consultants who want to charge exorbitant fees for all the belt classes. You can quickly train your internal folks to become Green Belts, and using the train-the-trainer concept, train future Green Belts.

Certifications are varied and differ from company to company. Insist on references from the consultant and examples of successful projects and tools used in the methodology. There are hundreds of tools that could be used in the lean six sigma process. There are about thirty to forty that are used most frequently. Ask which tool your tools your perspective consultant uses. Ask if they have previous experience in your industry. Let them talk about their project failures. Ask what they learned from them.

8. In Lean Six Sigma a Charter is Critical

A written commitment between a Six Sigma team and the organization, the charter includes the business case, problem and goal statements, constraints and assumptions, roles, preliminary plans, scope, and the roles of participants in the project. This document states the scope of authority for an improvement project or team, and is approved by management. Periodic reviews with the sponsor ensure alignment with business strategies. Charters should be reviewed, revised, and refined periodically throughout the DMAIC process, based on data.

Tips:

- 1. Make sure the charter identifies the defect or the problem clearly.
- 2. Make sure there are plenty of metrics to measure when you have achieved your goals.
- 3. Investigate if there is valid data available now.
- 4. Get the project champion to endorse the charter and participate in the DMAIC process.
- 5. If you cannot measure something, don't.

9. Poke-Yoke

Poke-yoke is a term that means error-proof. Error-proofing is one of the holy grails of Lean Six Sigma projects. It means that because of the process improvement, it is now impossible for an error to occur. Examples are computer fields that automatically fill in based on other information entered, or an email that is automatically sent when an event occurs. Make sure you apply it to your purchasing transactions also.

10. Company Culture is Essential for Lean Six Sigma Success

This is a system of values, beliefs, and behaviors inherent in a company. It is the most critical aspect for Lean Six Sigma Success. The company culture has a strong effect on business performance, so top management needs to define and create the correct culture in order to ensure optimum performance of Lean Six Sigma.

11. Why Supply Management Must Lead Change

No other department in an organization has more

dynamic issues to deal with than supply management does. Supply management is continuously challenged by changing global events and demands from both internal and external customers. My advice to supply management professionals is to lead the change (be a warrior) and not be a victim of change.

12. Analyze the Process Map Delays Then Brainstorm the Fixes

First do a process map. Teams should review the as-is/current-state process map delays such as, inventories, and hand offs. Have the team analyze or give the reasons for the delays or the whys, and then list them.   Discuss root causes if known, and list them right on the as-is process map. There may be multiple ones. If you can categorize them, sort them out.

Then establish the rules for the brainstorm session and solicit the team's ideas via a brainstorming session on overcoming the delays or fixes. Capture them, and list them right on the as-is process map.

This basic methodology works for many process improvement projects.

13. De-Mystifying Lean Six Sigma for Purchasing Professionals

Many supply chain and purchasing professionals are intimidated by Lean Six Sigma (LSS) and its proponents. Relax. It is just a disciplined approach to problem solving. LSS uses many tools that have been around for years; in many cases the tools have just been cleverly repackaged by consultants.

Decisions are data-based, disciplined and plodding.

Without top-down commitment, LSS is doomed to fail. Make sure you secure this executive commitment, and better yet make participation a strong criterion for individual performance reviews (raises). Projects should be selected by ROI (Return on Investment) and since much time and teams are required for a project, they must return or save at least $300,000 to qualify as a full blown LSS project.

Supply chain and purchasing professionals must be involved in sourcing the LSS consultant. Experience is critical and a proven track record of project success essential. Get references and insist on examples of work. Use a fixed hourly rate and make sure all developed training and projects remain your property. You can try to make the contract performance-based but many LSS firms will not agree to this. Make the goal to be self-sufficient internally within two years with all LSS training and projects.

Some LSS projects that have been done in purchasing and the supply chain are: Inventory cost, part obsolescence prevention, lead-time reduction, backlogs, unexpected orders, customer service internal and external, cost of schedule changes, transaction flows, cost of return product, and supply chain optimization. Many of these involve process mapping which is a type of flow chart that illustrates how things are done and identifies areas of strength or weakness.

LSS is not the only tool that can be used by supply management professionals for improvement. In my experience LSS should be used when the potential savings is great and you have some good data to analyze. If you do not have good data the LSS project will take even longer. If data is sparse, the Lean approach is much preferred which is highly visual, intuitive and does not require as much data.

Always Lean a process before you use LSS. By this I mean eliminate any redundant steps in the process that can be easily eliminated first. Reduce the number of variables in the process. Try to understand the voice of the customer (VOC) clearly before your start process improvement. Remember if the customer does not really care or value a process step; ask yourself, "Why are we doing it?"

Finally use Kaizens for straightforward less complicated projects. The kaizen approach is usually done by the work team using the process and strives to eliminate waste in the process. The new kaizen improved process should then be quickly implemented. Supply chain and purchasing professionals must take the leadership role in LSS, Lean and Kaizens. In my professional experience, the rewards of these approaches can be astounding. They do however require a measured and disciplined approach, and a commitment to not giving up.

11 METRICS

1.   The Amazing Success Of Pay-For-Skill Compensation Plans: Are Quality Improvements Hype Or Fact?

Pay-for-skill compensation plans have the highest success rate bar none among management innovation programs. Is it hype or fact? I say fact!

A pay-for-skill compensation plan raises the pay of existing employees for acquiring new work skills and knowledge. Companies develop a continuous learning environment to teach employees more skills. As they advance up the ladder to each higher skill level, their pay increases.   A recent Towers Perrin study confirms that these plans not only work but can revolutionize product quality gains.   According to the study average productivity increases exceeded 40% and customer product complaints dropped by over 60%. My own extensive survey of over 200 pay-for-skill plans revealed that measured product defects were reduced by as much as 50%. The American Compensation Association reports very similar results. These pay plans are becoming more accepted but remain widely misunderstood. Despite these solid numbers skeptics still are wary of such plans. These critics believe much of the so called gains of these systems have not been closely quantified and the startup costs are prohibitive. They argue that more money should be invested in automation. My survey disproves these reservations.

The plans focus on uplifting the knowledge and the intellectual caliber of the workforce. They have some unique characteristics that lay the foundation for their uncanny achievement record. They are idiosyncratic. Most organizations custom-design them for their unique situation. The companies who reported the greatest success were already on board with so called "soft skills" such as employee involvement, empowerment, and participative programs.

The evidence repeatedly shows that the overwhelming majority of companies are committed and pleased with their pay-for-skill compensation plans. Of the 200 companies sampled only 2 (1%) stated that they would not implement the system again or were greatly dissatisfied with their plan. Superior quality, increased job flexibility, improved productivity, better employee growth, and leaner staffing were the most cited benefits.

If all this data points towards solid gains why all the skepticism? The cultural transformation to a participatory style and the need for strong top management commitment must come first (85% of the firms strongly agreed with these statements). This is no easy sacred cow to turn into a sacred steak! Most survey respondents (70%) reported that establishing trust with employees was the toughest ideal to realize. Implementation is brutal and requires tremendous time and resources. Many respondents cited an intensive one to two year implementation plan. Increased education or training costs ranged from $5000-$17,000 per employee. Numerous firms reported however that after these initial high training costs, the continuous learning costs dropped considerably. Over 60% of the companies reported using innovative and less costly self, online or programmed learning techniques in the later plan stages. Initial drops in productivity and output (up to 5-25%) were broadly reported during this "teething" phase which varied from 1 to 6 months. After two years measured productivity gains ranged from 30% to 90%. No other true management innovation plan requires such a long term incubation period and such a costly start up curve. This scares many firms away from the attempt and fuels skepticism that such a high-priced plan would ever pan out.

The burden of increased communication was the most noted bottleneck during the beginning phases (cited by 64% of the respondents). This road block is not new news. A recent Business Week survey reveals that less than 25% of employees feel that their bosses communicate company goals well to them.

The real heart of the pay system is the continuous learning and training process. Employees have an opportunity to progress up various skill levels or steps such as Technician1-2-3-4 etc. The more successful plans required employee skills pre-assessment before implementation and mandated universal participation. Total labor costs (direct and indirect) fell on average 15% of the total cost of goods and services being produced. Over 50% of the surveyed firms cited staff position reductions as exceeding expectations.

For most companies in the early stage the corporation became a skill-university. At startup (3-12 months in range) as much as 10-15% of total work hours were devoted to learning. This strong investment reassured employees that leadership was sincere about this process and in it for the long haul. Many firms did report that once the plans were established learning times were significantly reduced and innovative techniques more widely used and accepted.

Since employees and management collaboratively work on the design of the system, joint learning about job content and the nature of the business occurs simultaneously. Most other corporate innovations do not have such a personal benefit for the employee or a very well-defined path to achieve the end result. Philosophies such as total quality management (TQM) are broader in scope and are usually implemented to improve competitiveness. Their direct impact on employees is often difficult to define. Overall business effect can be notable with TQM, but employees may view it as another management "program" that like old soldiers will eventually just fade away.

The real power of pay-for-skill pay plans is that they have an immediate, personal, and nurturing impact on every employee. Implementation demands that management become beginners again and really understand exactly what employees are doing and what skills should be valued and rewarded with more pay. Cash or pay does motivate, a lot, no matter what the organizational behaviorists say to the contrary. Unfortunately many current management teams are quite clueless about what is really necessary in order to complete a particular job or task in a company. This proliferates our cycle of mindless corporate downsizing and the short-sighted outsourcing of employee skills and knowledge. The total immersion type approach of pay-for-skill plans engenders a much deeper search for better quality than any other program.

My survey revealed great news for companies that have TQM programs or who were ISO 9000 certified. The quality gains at these firms were statistically much more significant. The defect level dropped as much as 30-50% more than at companies without such prior programs. These preceding efforts helped kick start the startup stage (20-60% shorter in duration at such firms). Quality endeavors imply a commitment to long term survivability of the company and usually require specific examination of job tasks, work instructions, and inter-department relationships. In most quality committed firms management already possesses a good working knowledge of what it takes to perform a job or task in the organization. Pay-for-skill plans further refined this understanding and helped raise the quality level even more than anticipated. (This was cited by over 74 respondents)

One cannot underestimate the power of employee belief in such systems! With pay-for-skill pay plans, many employees are encouraged to not only learn, but teach their job design to others. They are usually quickly rewarded for increasing their skills. The immediacy of rewards, constant reinforcement via continuous learning, and the fact that management becomes more knowledgeable about job design and content, and thus more sensitive, explains the almost universal success of pay-for-skill plans.

The startup phase of a pay-for-skill pay plan is extremely challenging and frustrating for all parties. My survey uncovered the best start up methods. The plans require Sisyphean like efforts for implementation. Nothing worthwhile on the shop floor or corporate hallways is easy. Pay-for-skill plans demand the total indomitable commitment of an organization.

The survey listed the following start up methods as crucial in order of importance:
1.   Visit other pay-for-skill companies and start slowly with a small pilot plan.
2.   Conduct team building exercises and pre-assess the skills of the workforce.
3.   Plan and execute an intense communication program about the plan.
4.   If a strong quality program is in place use its principles to help re-enforce the pay-for-skill plan.
5.   Have clear and deliverable goals for the compensation

plan.

Pay-for-skill compensation plans are the most successful corporate innovations available. Their outstanding results have been documented repeatedly. Skeptics need to re-visit their concerns. Implementation requires good old fashioned perseverance. The quality gains can be significant especially if TQM is already in place. The plans emphasize people investment rather than people cutbacks. By utilizing the above now proven techniques during the tough startup phase, you can guarantee the smooth implementation of this powerful competitive tool and gain quality preeminence. Now that you are up to the challenge what are you waiting for?

2.   Leading Edge Metrics

Most purchasing professionals are familiar with the usual quantifiable supplier metrics and measures. Sophisticated computerized tracking programs exist to measure these traditional performance factors. There are nontraditional supplier metrics/activities that can help not only to rate a supplier, but also to build much stronger supplier relationships.

First, you can learn a lot about a supplier by visiting its sites and just observing the cleanliness of the plant, morale of the employees and overall sense of urgency of the operation. For most purchasing professionals the challenge is finding the time to conduct these visits and conducting them skillfully. A planned and disciplined site visit schedule can help overcome this obstacle. Every site visit should be documented and have a report filed for future comparison. It should always include the subjective impressions of the visiting purchasing professional.

How a supplier performs in disaster recovery (yours) provides an invaluable lesson of their commitment to you. We once had an electrical supplier lead the effort to restore power to one of our chemical plants after a devastating hurricane. The employees at the plant still marvel about how well they performed. These out-of-the-ordinary efforts should result in strong recognition to the supplier and possible increased sourcing from them. It can lead to another strong relationship-building activity of pre-planning for possible disaster-recovery with not one but multiple suppliers before they happen. Often vulnerabilities can be anticipated and dealt with appropriately.

Participation in process improvement efforts, such as Lean Six Sigma, is another strong builder of supplier commitment. Supplier input and suggestions to specifications changes for a part or service are invaluable. Many suppliers are eager to provide suggestions to help improve your process. Turnabout is fair play and you should participate in their process improvement and process-mapping efforts with their products, especially those that you purchase.

We once had a supplier increase the life of a critical part that cost us $35,000, from 30 days to 250 days. It did take two years of painstaking work and experimentation. Eventually, because we dramatically reduced the dollar value of our purchases (with the supplier's help), we hired the supplier as an ongoing technical service consultant. They had learned so much about our production process and now had the capability of providing invaluable insights.

Sharing of R&D efforts and data systems is another high level of cooperation that can lead to mutual benefits. Obviously this requires an extremely high level of trust and collaboration. It quickly reveals the IT capabilities of the supplier and its ability to respond to your needs. Many suppliers are often willing to share industry and market research with customers along with forecasting techniques. Take advantage of their expertise in these areas.

These types of relationship building metrics/activities can lead to dramatic gains for both the supplier and the purchasing professional. A purchasing professional needs to realize that most are not quick fixes but require a concerted and tough long term effort. The payback can be dramatic.

3. Some Non-traditional Supply Chain Metrics 1
- The number of preferred suppliers under long-term contract.
- The number of supplier-alliance relationships.
- The number of single-source parts, commodities, services.
- The number of suppliers providing onsite service.

· The number of new products or design reviews that suppliers participated in on a team.

The one that probably has the most value is having suppliers who participate in design for six sigma for a new product or service. They provide an invaluable outside perspective.

4. Some Additional Non-Traditional Metrics 2

· The number of transactions processed directly by the end-user.
· The number and dollar-value of mutual cost reductions with suppliers.
·The number and dollar-volume of purchase-card purchases or electronic purchases.
· The number of cross-functional teams on which purchasing professionals are contributing members.
· The dollar value on continuous-replenishment stocking plans.

The cross functional team approach is invaluable in the strategic sourcing of products and services. Internal customers can often provide input on streamlining the process map and reducing non-value adding work.

5. Keep Metrics Visible, Clear, And Simple. (VCS)

Show folks how you are doing versus your metrics. Use pictures and graphics. People can relate to them much better. Spreadsheets are not very publicity friendly. Don't be shy with graphs, and always display them professionally. Keep the radar gun on the process and suppliers. Let other folks see the results, good and bad. One of the fundamental tenets of Lean is visibility.

6. Aim High with People's Standards and Expectations

Set the standards of performance for yourself and your people high. Expectation-setting is critical to success. Reward outstanding performance, not average performance. Encourage supply management professionals to become experts in a market, industry, or supplier group. Most of all encourage them to know your business, the cost drivers, and the end-customer's needs, and strive to exceed them. This is the only way to get company-wide credibility and respect.

7. On Time Delivery Must Be Measured Differently

The traditional way to measure this is a percentage of deliveries delivered on time. Enhanced methods to measure this include separating components into the A-B-C categories. Strategic materials must arrive on time. The non-strategic material deliveries should be tracked differently. Their purpose is an ancillary supporting role. More leeway in deliveries can usually be tolerated. Many companies break delivery performance down into these A-B-C categories with different percentage goals in each category. One non-traditional measurement is the number of "no hitch" or perfect deliveries. This means a smooth delivery with zero redundancies and no extra non-value adding work. Deliveries that require any type of extra process time, administrative work, or quality waiver must be tracked and examined. Alternate approaches can easily be developed from the lessons learned from these less than perfect deliveries.

8. Inventory reduction measurements that can help supply chain managers.

Measure improved inventory accuracy, labor hours saved taking inventory, elimination of racks, shelves, and materials handling equipment, and reduced maintenance costs. Don't stop here. Many suppliers readily agree to hold materials on a consignment basis. This is a valuable cost-avoidance and cash-flow improvement. Whenever possible, drive to get agreement to pay on consumption. Also, track reductions in supplier inventory. This will help them reduce or hold down their costs to you. Measure inventory committed to by suppliers and value of materials that are now on consignment or on pay-on-consumption systems. Make note of the various functions or departments that are outsourced. Obtain realistic estimates of the amount of inventory and overhead that would have been required to support these activities if they were not outsourced.

9. Visibility And Appreciation Of Purchasing Count. Some Unique Measurements.

Measure the number of cross-functional teams that purchasing participates in and leads. These can be broken down into three general arenas: design, process, and administrative. Also, keep a record of the number of times other departments come to your department to seek input, advice, and basic participation on strategic planning. Track the number of suppliers that add value to your products at the design stage and the results of their efforts.

10. Strategic Performance Metrics for Purchasing and the Supply Chain

"Unless you have clear goals you are a nomad, not an explorer."

Many purchasing organizations struggle with the appropriate metrics to use. They often neglect strategic metrics and favor more tactical and transactional ones. This type of approach just encourages a stereotypical view of purchasing that is traditional and bureaucratic. Emphasizing strategic metrics encourages a different image of purchasing and, more important, strategic-like behaviors by purchasing professionals.

One key strategic metric is the number of supplier alliances. These should be not many, and ideally be limited to suppliers that have a key impact (significant dollar spend percent) on your total cost of goods sold. Often 20% or fewer of your suppliers account for 80% of the spend. The emphasis should be on suppliers that can differentiate you or give you a distinct competitive advantage. Characteristics of such alliances should include long-term evergreen contracts, participation in new-product design sessions, joint process improvement efforts, exchanges of executives, direct electronic links and cycle-lead time reduction.

Another measurement should be the number and percentage of suppliers that are certified: ISO 9001, ISO 14001 etc. These are not guarantees that a supplier is perfect, but they do indicate that they are pursuing excellence and at least have an understanding of their processes and how they perform their work. This is a significant first step in any joint supply chain process improvement effort. If the supplier is dedicated to its own program of process improvement via Lean or Lean Six Sigma, joint cooperative ventures are more likely.

Besides purchasing having its own mission and vision statement that aligns with the corporate plan, leading-edge purchasing departments should have their own five-year strategic purchasing plan. Elements of this plan should include all future initiatives, projects, metrics, goals and resources needed.

A noteworthy area to include in the plan is professional development. Purchasing team members should be encouraged to get professional certification, become industry, not just materials experts, and improve their overall knowledge of the business. The most vital area, that is often neglected, is getting more knowledge of what is critical to the paying customer of your product or service. Purchasing professionals should have close ties with sales, marketing, marketing research and shadow them on customer calls.

Another strategic measure is to have a sourcing methodology and to constantly update it based on market and global conditions. A critical aspect of this methodology should be sourcing with cross-functional teams, use of the Porter five forces model when appropriate, and high visibility along with transparency during the selection.

Ideally these strategic metrics should be put on a corporate dashboard to be seen by all employees. Strategic metrics should also be the catalyst for developing a balanced scorecard for purchasing. Unfortunately purchasing often neglects strategic metrics and focuses of fire-fighting and tactical metrics. Strategy always trumps tactics and strategic metrics need to become a valued tool for all purchasing organizations.

12 E-PROCUREMENT

1. Make Transaction Experiences Super User Friendly Or Else It Will Fail.

Face it, internal folks view doing their own procurement transactions as an outright pain. Every effort must be made to make them simple, intuitive and painless. Catalogues must be super-simple. Catalogue content is a key. Time is of the essence to anyone buying. One of the reasons the Russian empire fell was not Star Wars but because so many people had to wait so long in so many lines in order to buy so few basically worthless goods. Waiting riles people up. Target a transaction completion for 30 seconds or less. If you can archive previous requisitions that folks can copy, cut and paste quickly into new ones by all means employ this tactic. Do not waste their time on busy work. Their time is valuable.

2. In E-Procurement Speed is Critical & Resistance to Change Fierce

Underestimating resistance to change and the end-user's need for ease-of-use has derailed many e-procurement projects. A strong component in this area is content quality and the details of the transaction.

End-users demand ease of use and they want to quickly find the items that they need. Companies need to realize that e-procurement is competing with the easiest method to buy in the minds of their end-users. Many end-users would rather pick up a phone, tell their supplier what items they want, charge it to a corporate purchase card, and hang up. Unfortunately, in many companies, this method is still faster than using the current e-procurement software. Any impediments to the fast purchase of materials will quickly turn off end-users and kill transaction volumes. Speed is king in the world of e-procurement. End-users also want powerful search engines to quickly find their items. If the content of the supplier catalog is poorly organized and the quality poor, end-users will quickly be frustrated by unfruitful searches and become non-users of the e-procurement system. In addition, special instructions that need to be given to suppliers about delivery or other issues can't easily be given with some e-procurement tools, or require additional end-user training, which raises the frustration levels.

Resistance to change for an e-procurement system is fierce but can be readily overcome with strong commitment to change management. This change-management process must be an integral part of any e-procurement installation.

Never underestimate the role resistance to change plays in any software implementation.

3. The Five Most Common Mistakes In Implementing E-Procurement:

- Not creating a comprehensive procurement strategy first or a plan that aligns with an e-business strategy and an e-procurement strategy.
- Putting the e- before procurement. Technology and e-procurement won't fix current unsound procurement practices.
- Not performing comprehensive strategic supplier sourcing first and failure to prepare suppliers for e-procurement.
- Not properly identifying materials-services groups and the proper e-procurement tool to use for these groups. Not assessing supplier capabilities, which include readiness for e-procurement.
- Underestimating resistance to change and the need for ease of use for end-users. A strong component in this area is content (catalogue) quality and the transaction details.

13 BROKEN WINDOWS

1. Why Broken Windows Management?

The biggest reason for using the Broken Windows Management method is its simplicity, speed and its success record. People have a very low tolerance for long drawn out and methodical processes to improve work. The Broken Windows Management approach offers a quick and more rational approach to improving work. It works best when the people who actually do the work participate in and make the changes. This foundation in fixing employee dissatisfiers adds to its credibility. It is a full speed ahead solution to small improvements in quality of work life and processes.

Who Does the Work - Advantage

Employees should point out the issues and problems; they can also participate in fixing them. It can be one of the more participatory management strategies.

Is the Broken Windows Management the Right Tool?

Using the Broken Windows Management in an organization that is not ready for it is a losing proposition. Employees must be convinced that management is serious about the theory and backs up the theory with visible results.

1. Get the small projects done quickly
2. Don't be afraid of being overwhelmed, keep fixing and attacking the employee issues.
3. Get leadership on the firing line or on the shop floor including executives.
4. Get as much intelligence about what employees want as you can handle.
5. Fix things!

Does Broken Windows Management Work?

First off the track record of many management flavors-of-the-month is abysmal. Although the broken windows theory has been used in law enforcement and is controversial, my main recommendation for using it is t the following:

☐   It actually fixes the issues that employees' want fixed.

☐ It is highly visible and can be easily tracked.

☐ No expensive consultants or theories are involved.

☐ It does include improving quality of work life and morale.

☐ It improves the entire organization's skill is fixing things.

☐ It builds employees trust in management.

I cannot honestly point to reams of data or studies that a\say that it works. I can only say that out of many management theory options or fads it is one of the most practical and uncomplicated. I urge my readers to give it a try.

2. Broken Windows Management for Business Review by Kelly Barner Buyers Meeting Point

One of the most powerful things you can do with broken windows management is to empower your employees to fix their own issues whenever possible." (p. 35)

In his fifth business book (seventh overall) Dr. Tom DePaoli takes broken windows theory and combines it with liberal doses of lean methodology and his own no-nonsense approach to process improvement. While this is not a long book, just 70 pages long, it is a working book. This is emphasized by the pages at the back that are specifically designated for "Doodles, Notes, and Ideas."

Broken windows theory is an approach to establishing and maintaining urban stability by addressing minor crimes and disturbances. Simply put, the idea is that if you fix the broken windows, the effect that has on the environment will lead to reductions in larger scale crimes. Introduced in 1982, broken windows theory has been applied a number of times, perhaps most notably by Mayor Rudy Giuliani and Police Chief Bill Bratton in New York City. It was also covered by Malcolm Gladwell in his book The Tipping Point.

Dr. Tom takes the theory and focuses on the role it can play in empowering employees by working with them and through them to improve an operation. As he wrote, "The more you fix problems, the more employees will trust you." (p. 9) But while these changes may be minor in the grand scheme of things – access to food/drink, better parking, conveniently managed supply inventory – the reason for all of it is improved team cohesion and results.

There are two ideas that I particularly like:

Anticipatory maintenance: "Instead of having maintenance people wait around and wait for something to break, encourage them to seek out issues that bother employees and work with employees to improve them. This is beyond preventative maintenance, where you maintenance workers team up with the employees and find out the real issues that can make their quality of work life better." (p. 31) This is a great application of broken windows management. It signals the importance of time and effort, and positions every member of the team as a valuable contributor. Since no situation is ever perfect, there is always an opportunity to make improvements. Allowing employees to make decisions about how to use that time leverages their unique perspective and sets the expectation that everyone be productive at all times.

Non-value vs Value-Adding steps: "Clearly identify the process-cycle time, delays, handoffs, and any inventories, and try to differentiate between non-value and value adding steps." (p. 19) One of the areas where Dr. Tom's lean experience really shines is through process discussion and improvement. And as detailed as these processes can be, teams should understand the different kinds of steps that make them up. Not all steps add value – but not all *steps* need to add value. By understanding the difference, management teams can focus their attention and measurement efforts where they will generate the best return.

If you are a hands on manager looking for a way to improve the performance of your team and operation, this is a great book to pick up over the summer. It is deceptively thought-provoking and actionable for its short length and will help you restore focus to the little things that are really the big things.

ABOUT THE AUTHOR

Dr. Tom DePaoli is currently the Management Program Director at Marian University in Fond du Lac, Wisconsin. He is the Principal (CEO) of Apollo Solutions (www.apollosolutions.us), which does general business consulting in the human resources, supply chain, transformation, and Lean Six Sigma areas. The company was founded in 1995. He retired as a captain from the navy reserve after over thirty years of service. In other civilian careers, he was a supply chain and human resources executive with corporate turnaround, transformation experience, and Lean Six Sigma deployments. He has worked for over ten major companies and consulted for over 150 organizations throughout his career. Some of his consulting projects included: information systems projects, reengineering organizations, transformation, e-procurement, e-commerce, change management, global sourcing, and negotiating. His industry experience is in the chemical, paper, pharmaceutical, IT, automotive, government, consumer, equipment, services, and consulting industries. He has published extensively in journals, magazines, blogs, and books.

> Twitter = Dr Tom DePaoli@DrTomDePaoli.com
> Email = drtomd@gmail.com
> Website = www.apollosolutions.us

His other published books (all available on Amazon.com) include: Common Sense Purchasing, Common Sense Supply Management or Tales from the Supply Chain Trenches, Growing up Italian in the 50's or How Most of Us Became Good Wise Guys, Jayson and the Corporate Argonauts—the Quest for the Golden Fleece of Transformation, Kaizen Kreativity (OOPS!), Broken Windows Management in Business, Sydney the Monster Stops Bullies.

INDEX

Dr. Tom DePaoli

44186043R00095

Made in the USA
Lexington, KY
08 July 2019